Endorsement for
I Give This to You Lord!

After reading Darlene Link's book, I found a deep truth there that a person will find difficult or impossible to understand unless they have been through it; it's called "Suffering!" Without going into the depth of it, my wife Doris (of 66 years together) and I have known suffering after losing two of our three sons to death. Once a person has been through it, they will never be able to forget it!

No one has ever suffered as Jesus Christ suffered. Jesus was beaten, spat upon, mocked, nailed to a tree, had a spear thrust into His side until it pierced His heart and bled to death. If there was ever anyone qualified to comment on suffering, it was Jesus Christ. Yet, He says: If we suffer with Him, we will also reign with Him (2 Timothy 2:12). The key to reigning through suffering is to love enough to do what Scriptures tell us to do: "Looking unto Jesus, the author and finisher of our faith, who for the joy that was set before Him endured the cross, despising the shame, and is set down at the right hand of the throne of God" (Hebrews 12:2-3).

Darlene's captivating story will open the door to this mystery to whomever has the will and courage to read and pursue it. The key to entering this truth is to deny and humble ourselves; enter into the suffering that has been set before us; turn this over completely to God, and He will help us to turn our suffering into Joy.

—**Deacon Fred Williams, EdD,** *St. James Catholic Church, Gadsden, AL*

***

Darlene has written a wonderful and personal testimony of a difficult and challenging time in her life. In the process of suffering with a debilitating medical condition, she diligently sought for answers to her dilemma.

In this book she writes about her struggles to find answers as she seeks doctors' appointments, tests, and prescriptions to ease her pain. The doctors listened and did all they could professionally to assist her.

In her pursuit of an answer to resolve her medical issues, she trusts in her faith and calls upon the Lord Jesus Christ to bring a miraculous healing in her life. Her story is a testimony to God's presence and power in her life. She shares what is possible for anyone who calls upon His name.

—**Pastor Jerry Cribb (Rtd.),** *North Carolina Conference of the United Methodist Church*

***

Darlene Link's story, *I Give This to You Lord*, from her miracle meeting of John to her miraculous healing, tells of amazing miracles all resulting from giving things up wholly and completely to God! I only wish I had the complete strength and faith displayed in this amazing book by Darlene Link. If you have any doubts about giving all of your situations, good and not so good, to the Lord, this book should help you realize the importance of giving everything up to God.

Darlene teaches us that it must be His way, not ours! God knows what He is doing and this book taught me that I have to trust Him to know what is best and that will always be His will. I give everything up to you Lord! This book is the proof in the pudding!

—**Richard Pettys, Jr.**, *Host at The 4 Persons Network Talk Radio, Attalla, Alabama*

***

One of the hardest things to write about is our own personal journeys. This writer, Darlene Link, has taken the time to show us how complicated life can be and how there is only one real hope; that is learning to live a life of complete Faith.

I enjoyed reading, *I Give This to You, Lord,* because I could relate to her journey. At times, it made me cry. I believe readers will find a newfound hope after reading about her life and her testimony in God's promises.

—**Raymond Macon,** *Actor at Casting Companies, Stand-In, Walk-On, and Background Actor for 100+ media projects. Teaches writing and acting for camera courses*

***

I Give This to You, Lord, is a wonderful read. It's the true life story of Darlene Link, a typical American wife and mother, who becomes so much more by allowing God to work in her life. While Darlene's experiences may be extraordinary, they're a result of the living and true Lord answering her prayers for Jesus to use her to show His love to His children.

By her example, every Christian believer should sit down with a pen in hand and, like Darlene, reflect on the beautiful and miraculous tapestry of our lives that God has uniquely woven, if only we would say of our lives, *I Give This to You, Lord.*

—**Michele Cribb,** *Retired Methodist Pastor's Wife, and Educator*

***

Darlene Link's book, *I Give This to You, Lord,* is so touching in so many ways. It's a beautiful love story of a couple that is a devoutly loving Christian couple that are meant to be together and their love for their large, blended family. You will laugh, and you will cry.

Darlene's healing left her with a gift from God that has helped so many families and others. I suggest getting extra copies of this book to give to many who have lost hope. The power of her faith is so strong and unshakable. To be so sick for so long and to turn this over to God in deep prayers and faith and to be healed. This touched me so deeply because I've been there, so deathly sick and my parents being told there was nothing else that could be done and an all-night prayer chain began, and my fever broke the next morning. Prayer is so powerful, and I've seen Darlene's prayers for everyone that is in pain and feeling hopeless. God is using her voice to help touch those in pain and those who have lost hope. A book you'll read over and over again, and you'll feel the love of this devout Christian lady.

—**Bellann Fitts,** *United Methodist Member, Avid Reader*

I GIVE THIS TO YOU LORD

An Angelic Message Of His Healing

DARLENE M. LINK

Published by KHARIS PUBLISHING, an imprint of KHARIS MEDIA LLC.

Copyright © 2025 Darlene M. Link

ISBN-13:978-1-63746-357-4

ISBN-10:1-63746-357-X

Library of Congress Control Number:2025944651

All rights reserved. This book or parts thereof may not be reproduced in any form, stored in a retrieval system, or transmitted in any form by any means - electronic, mechanical, photocopy, recording, or otherwise - without prior written permission of the publisher, except as provided by United States of America copyright law.

All KHARIS PUBLISHING products are available at special quantity discounts for bulk purchases for sales promotions, premiums, fund-raising, and educational needs. For details, contact:

Kharis Media LLC
Tel: 1-630-909-3405
support@kharispublishing.com
www.kharispublishing.com

TABLE OF CONTENTS

Dedication ix

Preface xi

Introduction xiii

Chapter 1: Miracle Babies 15

Chapter 2: An Angelic Message 25

Chapter 3: Out Of The Mouths Of Babes 29

Chapter 4: Answered Prayers 37

Chapter 5: A Romantic Proposal 45

Chapter 6: Unity Of Two Families 53

Chapter 7: My Blessed Life Rattled With Illness 63

Chapter 8: Unusual Warning 75

Chapter 9: My Debilitating Disease Revealed 77

Chapter 10: Touched By The Lord 87

Chapter 11: A World With New Eyes 97

Chapter 12: God's Plan For Us 101

Chapter 13: Accepting Our Gifts From Jesus 113

Chapter 14: Surviving The Ohoopee River 139

Chapter 15: Understanding God And His Laws 151

Final words of encouragement 165

About Kharis Publishing *166*

DEDICATION

It is my greatest pleasure to dedicate this book to my husband, children and extended family. They have been wonderful throughout my diseases and all the challenges associated with them. I especially dedicate this book to my wonderful husband and best friend, John. Because of my diseases John has had to take on more roles than he bargained for when we were married. He was mom, dad, cook, maid, chauffeur, and all other titles to raise our seven children during times I could not step up to the plate. He was also my caretaker, and I'm mindful of the physical and emotional challenges he endured many times. Thank you, Honey, for being my rock. You got me through the ups and downs to get to where we are today. I couldn't have done it without you and your love.

I also want to take this time to thank our son, Noah, my husband John, and a dear friend Bellann Fitts, for reading and proofreading the book before sending it in for publication.

My deepest and greatest dedication and appreciation goes to our Lord. Through His miraculous healing, all of my family and friends were witnesses to the astonishing transformation of my body. I went from living in a critically ill body to living in a renewed energized body full of countless life purposes. All glory and praise of this book goes to my Lord and Savior, Jesus Christ!

PREFACE

This book was inspired by messages I received through the Lord's heavenly angels after my healing. In one of my stories, I reveal how one angel creatively got my attention when I was struggling with ideas on where to start. It still amazes me how clever the angels have been in getting my attention when I needed their assistance.

I also want to take this time to thank our son, Noah, my husband John, and a dear friend Bellann Fitts, for reading and proofreading the book before submitting it in for publication.

INTRODUCTION

I'm excited to share my healing as my "Testimony to the Lord." In this book I'll be sharing key events from my life journey. I'll share events before, during, and after my healing, as well as what led to this miraculous experience. Unexpected challenges can undoubtedly change a person's life. I'm hoping my experiences and family stories will give readers peace of mind knowing they or a loved one is worthy of our Lord's miraculous healing.

My life's journey has been multifaceted with wonderful fond memories I'll treasure forever, liberating independence, newfound love, an extended loving family, challenges of coping and surviving two horrifying overpowering diseases, and how my healing affected my life and those surrounding me. Then, one simple decision completely altered my being.

I'm sharing all of this, as well as how you or someone you love can also experience God's healing. God's healing opens our eyes to the beauty of the world around us. Being healed will most definitely bring a stronger relationship to God and His love. And as the angel said, "Write a book, it will help people." Each testimony is meant to inspire others to seek and receive healing. Praise Jesus!

CHAPTER 1
MIRACLE BABIES

Let me set the stage by sharing a little bit about myself and my life before these two debilitating diseases completely took over my body. First, the blessings of two miracle babies.

For many years in my youth, I desired to become a nun. I didn't mention this to many people, but I knew in my heart how I felt. My Roman Catholic faith was very strong, and I prayed consistently, but the more I babysat children, the more I fell in love with all of them. I was in my late teens when I decided not to become a nun because of my love and desire to have children. I just adored, and still adore, all children. I love how their brains are like sponges as they discover something new every day; how their love is unconditional, how they see the world with innocent eyes, and how their imaginations goes wild when they're exploring the blessings of nature. I knew I wanted a big family, and I knew I was ready to have children of my own soon.

I'd think of how I could make a difference by building a great foundation for my children, by molding them into God-loving individuals, not brainwashing them, but through exemplifying how our Lord wants us to live our lives. Parents can only show their children how they hope they'll be, but it's up to the children—after they've matured into adulthood—to make their own faith-based decisions. I hoped I'd be sending my children into the world with a wealth of knowledge about God to teach others, especially their own children. And after they found their true loves, they could, of course, shower me with lots of grandchildren, if having children is in their plans.

In my previous marriage, having children sounded great. Unfortunately, things didn't begin as I had originally imagined. After being married for nearly three years, I felt we were financially secure enough to start a family. Even though I was still young, I felt I was mature enough to handle this physical and spiritual responsibility. First, I wanted to visit my cardiologist to see what I needed to do to make sure my pregnancy was going to be a healthy one. Yes, I did say cardiologist and not OB/GYN.

THE COMPLICATION

When I as six years old, I had rheumatic fever. My temperature escalated to almost 106o and the high fever complicated my situation, giving me horrible hallucinations that seemed very real at the time. I could see hundreds of spiders crawling up my covers towards me. I let out a blood curdling, high pitched scream that I'm sure the neighbors could hear. My mother must have been terrified as she stumbled rushing to my aid. I'm sure the dreadful ear-piercing scream gave her many terrible visions of what could have been happening to me in just those few seconds before reaching me.

When she ran into my bedroom, she found me standing on my bed pushing my body up against the corner of the wall. I was looking down, horrified, attempting to get away from all the spiders she obviously couldn't see. I was trying to push them away by brushing them down and off my body. She swiftly leaned on the bed to pick me up as I continued screaming and crying. While she held my hot, fevered, petite body in her arms, I continued with this piercing wretched sound of horror. "They're coming

up, the spiders are coming up!" Still crying and screaming I told her, "They're coming up to get me, put me down, put me down!" When she put me down, they were still coming after me, this time crawling off my mother, crawling back up my legs and up my entire body. Then I screeched at my mother once again, "Pick me up, pick me up!" My mother was panic stricken as she lifted me off the floor and into her arms again. She told me years after this incident that when she grabbed the telephone book to look up the doctor's phone number she was in such fear that the pages seemed to go completely blank. My mother's anxieties and concerns grew stronger with every desperate second. Immediately, she reached out to our sweet English neighbor, Burl, who dialed the doctor's number for her. Meanwhile, my distress continued as I tried to push off the spiders I was still hallucinating from due to the high fever.

The doctor, who made house calls at the time, could hear me in the background and advised my mother of how to get my fever down immediately. Then, he told her he was heading to our house right away. By the time my mother took me out of the bathtub, my fever had already begun to decline, and the doctor arrived. He gave me an injection.

When I think about my distressful spider experience, I can remember seeing it clearly as if it just transpired yesterday. Oh, and if there's a question of my feelings towards spiders today, I'm not terrified of them as one would think after such a traumatic experience, but I'm not their number one fan either.

As a teenager, I began seeing a cardiologist because of heart-related complications from that illness. Many times, I'd have palpitations when doing physical activities, especially activities involving jumping or running fast.

When I first started seeing a cardiologist, he confirmed to my parents that I had Rheumatic Fever when I was six years old. The tests he ordered revealed this damage to my heart.

As a child I had a weak immune system, therefore developing strep throat, tonsillitis, or bronchitis quite often. Even though I was well taken care of by my parents, it seemed impossible to prevent my body from getting one of these horrible infections. My siblings, Mark and Jon were pretty healthy, but I missed more than half a year when I was in first grade due to multiple illnesses. I was left behind that year because of losing so much time in school. The following year I was much healthier, praise God.

Results of my tests showed damage to my mitral valve, which is located directly between the heart's upper and lower left chambers; in my case, the valve was leaky and unable to close as it should. Blood flowed backwards into the left atrium, as a result.

Having rheumatic fever would certainly explain the high fever and ongoing extreme arrhythmia I've suffered throughout the years. My palpitations were diagnosed as supraventricular tachycardia or (SVT). Also known as paroxysmal supraventricular tachycardia (PST). This is an abnormally fast heartbeat with rhythm ranging from 100 to 300 beats per minute.

During my high school years, the frequent palpitations prompted my cardiologist to excuse me from all gym activities and competitive sports. This news was heartbreaking to me, because I believe I could have been an athlete if I'd only had a healthy heart. I was built for sports, had a lot of energy, coordination, and motivation.

I had a couple cardiologists through the years and one told me, "Only you know how your body feels. Just listen to the signs it's giving you." He was right. I'd stop what I was doing if I started experiencing any abnormal issues with my heart. When I was feeling good, I was more apt to do things I enjoyed.

In addition to the heart complications, I had difficulty breathing (dyspnea). I didn't realize how easy breathing was until years later when another cardiologist put me on heart medication. I remember thinking, Wow, who would have known breathing could be so easy? I had no idea!

So, back to my cardiologist's appointment to see what he recommended me to do to protect my heart throughout my pregnancy. I began sharing my desires to start a new family. Immediately, I didn't like his facial expression nor his words. The doctor said with my palpitations and prolapsed mitral valve I would never be able to have children. I'm not sure if I had the best doctor at the time, although I know there are many innovative options these days. Thank God for medical advancements of the heart. The doctor told me I'd need to have open heart surgery down the road. He described the risks of my having a baby by saying, "You would most likely be fine carrying the baby, however, the delivery and aftercare of the baby would be too problematic." He expressed his concerns for my health and the strain of caring for a newborn. He wasn't sure if my body was strong enough to handle it.

This unfortunate news was devastating to me. I knew I was ready to have a baby and even if it weren't a large family, a baby or two would have certainly been a blessing. I hated hearing those words spill out of his mouth. I knew I would be a great mom and could offer so much love and care to my child(ren), but here I was expecting the doctor to give me strict instructions like avoid heavy lifting, keep off your feet, and six months into the pregnancy you may be required to stay in bed until the delivery. It was not a good day, in fact, I cried a lot following my appointment.

MY RESOLVE

After several sleepless nights, I decided I wanted to proceed with plans to have a child. I was a stubborn, nearly 22-year-old, and knew that I gave up becoming a nun to have a huge family. My husband supported me in my decision.

I warily thought about what the doctor said, and I thought of every excuse I could to make my goal viable. I planned on taking good care of myself by eating healthy foods and not doing a lot of lifting or doing anything unnecessary that could otherwise add more strain on my heart or jeopardize the full term of the pregnancy. The plan was to have my husband help me on nights I needed help, and I'd ask for help taking care of our baby on weekends, if needed, and I knew I would need to rest every moment I could, once he or she arrived.

DARLENE M. LINK

Now that I look back at what I did, I feel ashamed for being so stubborn and selfish. I wasn't thinking about how my parents or spouse would feel if I didn't survive. I was too busy playing the, "What if!" game. "What if" I survived and we had worried for nothing, instead of weighing the "What if I didn't survive?" What would that do to my motherless baby and my widowed husband? Of course, now I'm glad I did become pregnant, because I have my two beautiful miracle girls that I wouldn't trade for anything. But I was being selfish not to include the concerns of other family members. God was beside me to see me through the decision I made. Thank you, Jesus, for keeping me and the girls safe.

When I found out I was pregnant, I was concerned for our child. I made sure I did everything in my power to follow the book for a healthy pregnancy. I took good care of myself, but I know I took a big risk going against the doctor's recommendation.

I loved every moment of being pregnant. I enjoyed my baby's every movement, especially when we could watch this tiny lump rush from one side of my belly to the other side. We'd wonder, was that a foot, arm, or an elbow? I also didn't mind it when people asked if they could feel the baby move. I enjoyed letting family and friends feel the marvelous miracle of life inside me.

I learned all I could about the stages of a baby's week-by-week development during pregnancy. I knew there wasn't an exact science or textbook that could tell me exactly what to expect, since children are all individuals, but I did buy plenty of books to give me a good idea of what to expect at what age to give me guidelines to follow.

I took the Lamaze classes seriously. My husband went with me as my coach. In one class he fell asleep during a relaxing exercise and started snoring loudly. We all got a good laugh out of that, but I'm sure he was embarrassed.

THE DELIVERY

Delivery for me was not easy. I ended up with toxemia (preeclampsia).

WebMD states:
> ***Preeclampsia, formerly called toxemia, is when a pregnant woman has high blood pressure, protein in her urine, and swelling in her legs, feet, and hands. It can range from mild to severe. It usually happens late in pregnancy, though it can come earlier or just after delivery. Preeclampsia can lead to eclampsia, a serious condition that can have health risks for mom and the baby and, in rare cases, cause death. Women with preeclampsia who has seizures have eclampsia.***
> *https://wwwwebmd.com/baby/what-is-preeclampsia.*

The toxemia wasn't discovered until I arrived at the hospital for delivery. I was running a high fever, and my blood pressure was very high as well. I could feel my heart racing irregularly. The doctors' words and warnings went through my mind. Immediately, I began praying we both would be ok. My water broke when we arrived at the hospital; once that happens, contractions become stronger and harder to bear. When the nurse checked in on me, I was drenched in perspiration. She followed instructions to give me medication to lower my blood pressure and lower my fever. Unfortunately, the medication slowed down my contractions, delaying delivery time and putting more strain on my heart. I felt like I was on fire and asked for a fan. The nurse immediately brought one in for me. Hallelujah Jesus, I needed that fan!

My doctor was concerned for me; therefore, he instructed a nurse to keep a close eye on me. My contractions were hard for a miserable 12 hours. I knew this was not good for my heart. I could feel it pounding hard and fluttering too often. My husband came into the delivery room. Back then, some couples took pictures of the miracle of delivering their child, and we wanted to do so as well. My husband nearly fainted, but a nurse tended to him briefly. He was fine during the rest of the delivery, and able to capture some incredible magical photos.

When I heard the doctor say, "It's a girl!," I was so happy. To me it hadn't been important to know what our child's gender was prior to delivery, as long as it was a healthy baby. I prayed for a healthy baby, and she was a perfect 8 lbs. 5 oz., 21½-inch long, beautiful baby girl. Looking down at our gorgeous, newborn angel was the most pleasing surreal moment to me. I could never understand how any woman could forget the labor pain so quickly, until that moment. We took one look at what we had just brought into this world, and we were absolutely captivated by her beauty.

I searched in many baby name books for weeks before deciding on the name Desiree, but after seeing her, she didn't look like Desiree, which means "desired". Someone said it was also the name of Napoleon Bonaparte's mistress. The name seemed less attractive to me then. While my in-laws were visiting us in the hospital, my father-in-law said, "I've always liked the name Crystal." I looked up the meaning of Crystal and it meant, "flower of Christ". How beautiful. I liked the meaning and looked at her and thought she really did fit the name. My husband and I agreed, and that's how she became our Crystal. I also gave her my middle name, Marie.

I was in the hospital a while longer than other delivering mothers. It was nice to have the rest and I did get to meet some nice roommates during my stay. The nurses catered to Crystal, which I believe was another order from my doctor. Things are so different these days, nurses are kept so busy and hospitals are understaffed. I believe they are angels on earth who sacrifice so much to help others.

My husband and I decided I would be a stay-at-home mom. This would also help keep me healthier for our family. Other than having reflux, Crystal was an easy, happy baby. She slept well, and I rested when she slept.

THE SECOND ATTEMPT

My husband would help at home to keep me from being too exhausted, and about a year and a half later, I was pregnant again. Unfortunately, I lost our second child in the first trimester. It was a difficult time and I felt guilty thinking I had done something wrong. The doctor said it was nothing I did, there was just something wrong with the pregnancy and sometimes this happens. I really empathize with mothers who have lost their child, especially later into their pregnancy or shortly after the birth of their child. At any stage, it's a terrible loss. I'm sorry for anyone reading this who has lost their child(ren). Blessings for all of us that will someday unite with our little ones when we go Home. I never got to learn the gender of my second child, but I do know he or she will greet me when I arrive in heaven. I look forward to that moment.

Our third and last pregnancy produced a 9 lbs. 1 oz., 22-inch-long Stephanie. She was born just one week shy of three years after Crystal was born. I chose the name Stephanie because it sounded good with the name Crystal, and the French name Stephanie means "crowned in victory", which I also liked.

Delivery was extremely difficult. No toxemia/preeclampsia this time, but my heart rate was very irregular and out of control. I had extreme difficulty breathing. The doctor was concerned and scared for my life. I'll never forget the looks of concern on his face. During the delivery all I could think to do was to pray to God that our baby and I would be fine. "Oh Jesus, please spare me and our child." Thanks to answered prayers, our baby and I made it through the delivery, but not with ease.

When they wheeled me out of the recovery room and into my hospital room, the doctor visited me right away. He admitted I scared him, and he thought he was going to lose me. He said, "You have two beautiful healthy daughters, and they need a mother." Then he proceeded to say, "I can go in tomorrow and take care of it for you." He explained the process; "I would cut, burn and tie your tubes. I think this would be best for you." I thought briefly and knew it would be too great of a risk to attempt having another child and selfish to say the least. It would do no good to have another child if our children were to be motherless and my spouse a widower. I knew the doctor was right and said, "Yes, you can set it up for tomorrow." He said he would do it first thing in the morning.

Having multiple twins run in our family. My grandmother had multiple sets of twins and my cousin Annette only six days younger than me had three sets of twins. I mention this because I feel the Lord protected me from having twins and blessed us with our two healthy daughters.

Now, it was time for me to start thinking about them and our family's future. Thank you again Jesus, for Crystal Marie and Stephanie Ann (I gave Stephanie my confirmation name Ann).

Visitors came to see our new baby bundle Stephanie, who was not exactly a small baby by any means. During my first night's visit, my parents and godparents, Aunt Mary, and Uncle Bill, were talking, when without warning, I just burst into tears. I couldn't help myself; my emotions were overwhelmed. I apologized and briefly explained the procedure I'd be undergoing the following morning. I told them I knew it was the right thing to do. Everyone knew my dream of having a large family and graciously, with their words of wisdom, comforted me by saying all the right things. Both my godparents are now angels of Our Lord watching over me.

Unfortunately, life is unpredictable. After 16 years of being faithful and dedicated to my marriage, we were filing for a divorce. This was something I never in my life thought would happen, but this is the way things had to be.

CHAPTER 2
AN ANGELIC MESSAGE

THE ANGELIC VOICE

It was important in my heart to feel I was doing what God wanted me to do in life. I became very depressed and went into what felt like a black hole during the last few months before filing for a divorce. I'll confess, just before a decision was made about the divorce, and, for the first and only time in my life, I felt angry with God. I felt I was trapped in an unhealthy relationship. Don't get me wrong, I never would have had two beautiful children if our marriage was always troubled; it wasn't until the last two or so years of our marriage that things changed. I no longer had the desire to do the things around the house I normally did. I wanted to do nothing more than sleep. Our daughter Crystal said she remembers just climbing into bed with me so we could lie there together.

The only thing I really cared about was my daughters' well-being; nothing else mattered, and I started to feel dead inside. When we went out with friends, I would dress nice and became an actress to make things seem so perfect, but because of that, the divorce was such a shock to people on the outside; they knew nothing of what was going on inside behind closed doors.

One night when the girls were at their grandparents I really felt helpless. I left our bedroom where my husband was sleeping and went into another room at the opposite end of the house where I sat on the floor leaning up against the wall crying and pouring out the pain in my heart. Those days I would cry often when nobody was around, but this time I really felt I needed to let out the pain and I sobbed hard, losing my breath and gasping for air between sobs. I was thinking about my situation, and I felt trapped. Then I believe wholeheartedly the voice of an angel of God gave me this clear audible message; "You don't have to stay." It was like a light bulb went off in my head when I heard it. And I said softly out loud in amazement, "I don't have to stay? I do have a choice."

It took an angelic message interceding from God in this decision because He was watching the whole time and never left my side. When we think we are alone, we are wrong. God is always there by our side. We just need to pray and ask for guidance, and then pay attention to His messages and new paths He opens for us.

Here was a new path I could choose to go on, or I could stay on the same path where I was unhappy. I listened to God's plan and followed in His direction. I did get my marriage annulment through my church after the divorce was final. That was important to me.

Life is full of challenges and choices. We also have our own free will to do what speaks to us in our hearts, as long as what we decide is pleasing to God. He is the One we will be facing when our deeds are completed in this temporary home.

> ***Corinthians 2:14 But thanks be to God, who always leads us as captives in Christ's triumphal procession and uses us to spread the aroma of the knowledge of Him everywhere.***
> ***https://bible.usccb.orgbible/2corinthins2***

THE AWAKENING

After making this decision I started to think and worry about how I was going to tell the girls. I knew it would be hard for them to understand, because our situation was hidden from them, our friends, and our family behind closed doors. How do you explain this to children who love both parents? I could not explain our situation to them at this point to make them understand. When I did sit the girls down to tell them we were divorcing, it was one of the most painful and difficult things I've ever done to this day, but for me and my relationship with the Lord, it had to be done.

Then I started to worry about how to survive and give the girls all the things they needed. My faith was more critically important than ever before because I needed the Lord's guidance for this new path He prepared for us. I came out of my depression once I saw the light at the end of the tunnel.

I became a divorced mother of two gorgeous daughters when Crystal had just turned 13, and Stephanie was a week away from turning 10 years old. There's no doubt their father and I love our daughters and feel very blessed to have them in our lives.

God has blessed us with these two kindhearted ladies. Seeing their love for one another is beautiful to witness. Each has her sister's name tattooed on their feet. They said if anything ever happened to the other one, they would always be with them.

Immediately, I could focus on being closer to God again. I started to improve my appearance, to make myself feel better, and to make plans for our future. I was alive again and loving the Lord. I can be pretty determined when I need to be to get something done, and I was.

Life is one big classroom; we are always learning. Whether it's good or bad, it's a lesson. I've learned people don't know what happens behind closed doors, and for that reason, I would never judge anyone getting a divorce, despite how things look from the outside.

My main concerns then were to live a positive life. Some of my friends had a hard time understanding what had happened, and this made our relationships difficult for a few years. This hurt me and my children tremendously, but my focus had to be on the girls, getting a job, and finding a place to live. A couple of years were difficult, but time healed, and life got much better.

As for my friends and I, we are all close once again. In fact, my girlfriends and I have some great times. Every now and then we'd go to a restaurant for dinner or do something special together. During these times we shared our lives by catching up with each other. Even though I've moved 12 hours away, we still manage periodically to get together to discuss new developments in our lives, the lives of our grown children, and our grandchildren's lives. Before you know it, we will be adding our great-grandchildren's happenings into the conversations.

Once, when I was in a movie theater with one of my children, just a few rows down from us were four white-haired elderly ladies. These ladies were joking and carrying on like young children before the movie began. I heard one say, "So what are we going to do next week?" I don't know if they just got together once a week, or if they were working on a bucket list, but it was great to see these white-haired ladies enjoying life together as if they were teenagers. Seeing them reminded me of how my girlfriends and I are going to be some day when everyone's retired.

CHAPTER 3

OUT OF THE MOUTHS OF BABES

A good acquaintance of mine, John, was finalizing his divorce while raising five lovely children of his own. John was the CFO at a well-established optometrist practice in Delaware.

When a position in the contact lens department became available, John contacted me immediately to share the newly opened position. He said, *"If you're interested, you may want to get an application in, right away."* He continued, *"I don't think it's going to be available very long."*

I thanked John and told him I would be there first thing in the morning with my resume. John knew of my divorce and knew I was in search of a job and a place for myself and my two girls. So, in our conversation he also mentioned a house right next to the practice that recently became available for rent; the house was owned by one of the doctors at the practice. My initial thoughts were, *wow, wouldn't it be great if I got the job and the place right next door to the job?* He also told me he could get the keys to show me the house if I was interested in seeing it. I told him that would be nice, and I'd contact him when I was available to see the house. I was in the middle of packing at the time, and I needed to get a job first to afford rent expenses. Another fortunate thought crossed my mind, the girls' school was only a couple of blocks away from the practice and the house. What a perfect set up it would be if everything fell in place nicely.

Life is unpredictable; we can never assume its outcome. There really is a plan from God, and we just need to be aware of doors opening and paths we can follow. We need to trust in His plan for us. If I did get the job and the house so close to the girl's school, I'd know for sure God was watching me closely and He had His hands in this plan. Like I said, He's been there all along. If I didn't get the job and house, I'd know He'd have a better plan for us.

THE JOB

After dropping the girls off at school the following morning, I headed straight over to the well-maintained optometrist practice to fill out an application and hand deliver my paperwork. I didn't want to take any chances of losing this opportunity that could make a huge difference on my economic predicament.

Dressed professionally, I came into the practice also wearing a cordial smile and I gave a pleasant, "Good morning," and mentioned my interest in the position. After filling out the application, I handed the receptionist my résumé and three well-written reference letters. While observing the office, I noticed it was a very busy practice. The receptionist politely took my paperwork and informed me someone would be contacting me soon. When I got into my van, I prayed for God to guide me with this amazing opportunity. As far as I could see, this position would greatly impact our lives in a positive way. But God knows the future and knows if this is the right fit for us. So, in my prayer I didn't ask for the position, but I did pray that I would graciously accept His decision. After leaving, I tried to keep myself busy and maintain faith to accept God's plan.

The next day, a few hours after dropping the girls off at school, I received a phone call from the contact lens technician regarding my interest in the position. She asked if I was available to come in for an early interview the following morning. Of course, I made myself available and agreed to the interview time. Despite my exterior confidence, I was still a bit nervous.

In keeping my faith that the Lord heard my pleas for help and feeling this was His answer to my prayers, I kept my spirits up.

My interview was with the contact lens technician I'd be working under in that department. I was feeling comfortable with how it went after leaving. You know how once you leave an interview; you begin to replay the conversations through your head like a video: the questions that were asked and how you responded to them? I hoped I had appeared to be a qualified individual for them to consider. Before leaving the office, the technician let me know she had a few more interviews and would be contacting me soon. Waiting was the hardest thing with so much on the line.

The very next day, while stirring my steamy roast beef, green beans, carrots, and potatoes crockpot dinner, I received the call I was waiting for. I think I was more nervous than when I was in the interview. To my surprise, I was offered the position right there on the phone. I was expecting to have another interview, but one interview was even better. Holding back my excitement, I accepted the position. The technician and I spoke a little bit about the position before hanging up.

Immediately, I called John to thank him for giving me the lead on the position. I let him know I got the job. He was happy for me and congratulated me. Now that I had the job, it was time to see the house. I told John I was ready to see the house when he had time to show it to me. As desperate as I was to find a place, I still wanted to make sure it met the dynamics I was looking for to make the girl's transition more comfortable. John said he could get the keys and show me the house that night after he left work.

THE HOUSE

When I arrived, and at first glance, I thought this charming white Cape Cod home with a good sized screened-in front porch appeared to be perfect. It was small, but after a full tour of the home, I knew it was perfect for our needs. There were two bedrooms, one bath, a kitchen, a nice sized dining room, a small living room, the good-sized front porch, a backyard, and a basement. I was told all utilities worked fine. The washer and dryer were in the gloomy, creepy, old basement, but they were included and that was a good thing. I loved the home. I told John I thought it was the right fit for us and couldn't wait to make it ours.

The doctor who owned the home offered funds for paint and supplies if I wanted to paint any rooms. I was enthusiastic about giving the home relaxing colors for a more peaceful vibe. All the walls were boring, stark white. This I thought was a blessing, because I enjoy painting and I especially was thankful we could put our own touches on the place at no cost to me, other than my own labor, which I didn't mind at all. The girls chose a pale pink for their shared bedroom. Their selected color went well with their pink and white bedding and white metal-framed bunk bed. The top was a single bed, whereas the bottom was a double bed. Sometimes I would sleep with them on the lower bed to comfort them.

I selected a soft natural tannish color for the living room and dining room; for my bedroom I chose a gentle tranquil green, and the kitchen I kept pure white. It was a small kitchen so keeping it white gave the illusion of it looking larger. Choosing soft relaxing colors made it a comfortable quaint perfect little home for us.

When we moved in, we were able to bring our dog Dumplin. She had been my shadow for nearly 16 years. She was a miniature poodle and was so smart she could identify each of her many toys by name. Dumplin liked the place too; she had her own cozy spot in a basket with soft blankets we fluffed just for her. She had so much personality in such a small body.

MOVING FORWARD

When I started my new job, the starting time was perfect. I'd drop my girls off at school then headed to the optometrists' building which was only a couple blocks away from their school. I'd be at work with about 10 minutes to spare. Then, at the end of the school day the girls attended an after-school program for about 50 minutes before I came to pick them up and head to our nearby house. It all was indeed a great plan God made for our family. Thank you, Jesus! Isn't He wonderful!

Things took off to a fantastic start and I enjoyed what I was doing. This new position would help me in supporting the girls' needs, and I appreciated John's aid in directing me to this opportunity. What a blessing it was to feel secure again.

I became involved in a relationship with a man after my divorce. He was in my life for a purpose, and I am glad we shared the time we did together. I broke off the relationship though because I knew it wouldn't be a long term relationship. Although he adored my children, I was looking for someone that could be more involved in their lives.

John and I were very professional being acquaintances at the same office. After I ended my previous relationship, my daughter Crystal came to me and said, *"You know, Mom, when I'm with Mr. Link, I feel like I'm with you. You both have so much in common."* And there you go, *"Out of the mouths of babes."* Hmmm, I'm thinking, She's up to something. Later I found out John's daughter Ashley had a similar conversation with her dad. These two besties were scheming up something. It seemed as if they were welcoming the idea of us being more than friends, and them more than friends; they would be best friends and sisters, that is, if we were compatible and things worked out in their favor. Most would call this match making. Having just ended a relationship, I wasn't actively seeking a new relationship right away, however, when I started praying regularly to God for a partner, I'd ask Him to send me a man strong in his faith and one who would love me and love my children as his own. I also prayed for a man who was family oriented. I wasn't sure if I'd remarry, but I was hopeful God would guide a loving, religious, family man in my direction someday. I was very specific in my prayer for "Mr. Right."

Several months later, employees were selected from our optometrist office to participate in the Dover Mall Health Expo, which consisted of professional trades set up in the mall to recruit new customers/clients to their trade/business. Some trades had to compete with other local practices or businesses, which meant we needed to be on our game and interesting when we spoke with visitors at our exhibit. Some of the topics from our exhibit were our customer service, eyewear products, and benefits we offered our patients and customers.

John and I were very professional, so it was fun speaking to people independently. At lunchtime, other staff members relieved us to take a break. We had an hour, so we headed to the food court. I remember neither of us was very hungry at the time, but we were thirsty from all our sales pitches.

I noticed John seemed a little nervous, which was not like him at all. He's usually a very confident man. Shortly before going back to our exhibit, John asked me if I would be interested in getting a cup of coffee or maybe dinner afterwards.

Now, about a month prior to this question, John had enough courage to ask me out on a date. He called me to see if I'd go to dinner and a movie with him. I'm sure it hurt his ego and confidence when I turned him down. I told him I was afraid of hindering our girls' good friendship, should something not work out and that I'd recently ended a relationship.

I took my time before responding this time. I thought about Crystal's remark that when she was with John she felt like she was with me because we had so much in common. I knew she liked him and was comfortable with the idea of us dating. I thought a moment longer, *hmmm...a cup of coffee can't hurt, and I am sure we will be hungry after we are done with the Expo. It will give me a chance to sit one-on-one with John to get to know him.* When people are simply acquaintances, there is a minimal amount of information you know about each other, but I was thinking if I accepted this innocent offer, it would give a more in-depth view of who John really was. I could see he was a great father and a successful businessman, not to mention he was a very attractive Italian man with his olive tone complexion, jet black hair, and a neatly trimmed black mustache and beard. Another very important factor was he was a church going man.

It was a Friday, which landed on their father's weekend. I knew he would be picking them up after school, so I didn't need to worry about them that night. So, I told John, "That would be nice." I could see he was relieved. He seemed more upbeat when we went back to our exhibit. It must've been hard for him to ask someone out who had already turned him down.

When we were finished with the exhibit, we packed up and traveled in our own vehicles to a friendly family chain restaurant just down the highway from the mall. I can only imagine what was going through his mind when he was driving to the restaurant. I know for myself; I was getting nervous, excited, and then I started second-guessing my decision. *Is this the right thing? What if it doesn't work out? How will this affect the girls and his children? How will it affect our co-worker relationship?*

We arrived in the parking lot, met in the middle and walked together to enter the restaurant. John opened and held the door for me. His father taught him to be a gentleman, a great quality I wish more men shared.

As I entered the restaurant, I felt different emotions rushing through my body. I'm sure he was experiencing similar emotions. We could possibly be moving forward to a different level of friendship. I was nervous, yet cautious.

PRAYERFUL MESSAGES

Many have not accepted God's path because of fear, insecurity, never being raised in knowing our Lord, anger towards God for one reason or another, not believing in something they can't see or put their hands on, and the list goes on. But I know this, if you don't follow His plan and miss an opportunity, He will prepare another one for you to hopefully follow. It's up to us and "our free will" to open our hearts. Then, step back to look at what's happening in our lives to see what's available to us when something new comes in our direction. Not every new opportunity is God's plan; we must evaluate the messages and pray about them. If something falls through and we don't get something we prayed for, we must believe it wasn't what

God wanted for us. Pray for guidance and accept the outcome. And we should never forget to thank the Lord when our prayers are answered. God has our interest at hand and will not lead us down a bad path. We make the moves so it's up to us to think clearly if a path really is in our best interest. ***Having a strong, clear, honorable faith is extremely critical in our walk with the Lord.***

CHAPTER 4
ANSWERED PRAYERS

As I said, the restaurant John selected was family friendly and I loved his choice. I was elated that he didn't suggest an elaborate romantic restaurant with candles and soft music. I don't think I would have been comfortable chatting in such an intimate environment with someone I've been good acquaintance with for several years. He chose wisely, for me.

John and I first chatted a little about how the day had felt long, but successful, then a little more about the practice and how much I'd been enjoying my job. After working there for quite some time, it was like having a new family. Everyone was so nice.

When the waiter took our order, I was a little nervous and made sure I didn't order anything crunchy or sloppy.

We were quiet for a moment, then John turned the conversation to our children, especially how funny our girls were trying to play matchmakers. We laughed and discussed how they are such great friends. Then we both opened with discussions about our children and briefly about our divorces, then we shared more private conversations regarding our childhood upbringing.

This is just a rundown of our conversations as we engaged deeply in listening to each other's stories.

JOHN'S CHILDREN

John's five children, oldest to youngest:

Ashley was 12 years old at the time of the divorce. She was the first of three adopted children from John's previous marriage, prior to he and his wife having two of their own biological children. Ashley was just a few days old when she was adopted.

John III was the second child adopted when he was nine months old. At the time of the divorce, he was nine years old.

Michael, the youngest and third adopted child, was only four months old when he was adopted. He was seven years old at the time of the divorce.

Noah was the first biological child born. He was four and a half years old during the time of the divorce.

Hala was the second biological child and the youngest of the five children. She was 18 1/2 months old at the time of the divorce.

**Best Friends now Sisters
Crystal and Ashley**

JOHN'S CHILDHOOD

John's father was the youngest of 12 children. Unfortunately, his grandfather passed away when John's father was only nine years old. His father had three sisters who became nuns at Saint Rose Catholic Church in Lima, Ohio. They served their entire lives as Sisters of Charity.

John's father is German and served in the US Navy, where they call themselves the "Tin Can Sailors". Then his father worked for the Dover, ILC Program for NASA in Delaware. His father played an important role in the quality control inspections for NASA's astronauts' spacesuits, including the first men who set foot on the moon. His father had to clear all safety inspections prior to an astronaut's journey to the moon. The suits couldn't even have so much as a single pin hole in them, or it could cost an astronaut's life. To me it sounded like an interesting job, but indisputably one that came with great responsibility, dependability, and precise perfection to confidently clear the spacesuits' safety.

John's father had a terrible accident falling a great distance from a roof his father and a friend were replacing. His injuries were quite serious. John left college at The Ohio State University so he could help his family financially and emotionally, and also to continue his college education close to home.

Once he recovered from the accident, John's father decided to become an electronics teacher at Hodgson Vocational Technical School. It was a school of trades for high school students from surrounding schools. Students would commute half a day at their high school, then learn a trade the other half of the day at Paul M. Hodgson Vocational Technical High School in Glasgow, Delaware. This news was especially interesting to me because I went to that school. I was in the Medical Office Assistant program for three years. I was surprised to hear who his father was because I remembered his father quite well and saw him frequently. He was a sweet man with a great smile that made others smile. He was well respected by his students and colleagues.

DARLENE M. LINK

John's mother loved her Italian heritage. She was the youngest of seven in her family. She enjoyed cooking like her mother and Nonna, (Grandmother). His mother and Nonna would teach John and his siblings how to cook Italian style meals and bake amazing Italian desserts. His mother also cooked and invited the astronauts to their home. How many families could say they had the first astronauts eat at their house?

His mother used to manage the Blue Hen Mall in Dover, DE. John said he loved it when his mother worked there, because he used to visit her for lunch so they could walk around the mall to get some exercise.

His mother was the rock of the family. She adored her kids, grandchildren, and the sweetheart she married. She was an excellent Bridge player and used to teach it. She also was an artist who taught the skill to others.

John's mother delivered four children. John's sister Michele is almost three years his senior and his brother Eric almost three years his junior. John's tone softened when he spoke about his slightly older brother Vincent, who had passed away in the hospital shortly after he was born. John explained, "This was very hard on my mother and the family." Interestingly, John's parents were going to name their son John Vincent, Junior, after his dad, but when they were informed he wasn't going to survive they decided to name him Vincent John. However, when John was born, they named him John Vincent, Jr. to carry on the family name. Before Vincent was born, John's mom decorated the baby's room in purple tones. This was her favorite color, but after Vincent's passing, she never wanted to have purple around. It became a sad color for her when she saw it.

John's childhood appeared to me to be a healthy one; the kids had chores, they went to church together, made meals together, enjoyed camping and boating, played sports, cards and more. Sure, kids will be kids, but as for John, he was the near perfect kid anyone could ask for. He started a prayer group in his high school in the late 70's. This new "club" was held in a classroom where students could go at a certain time of the day to pray to whomever they wished without interruption. Many students sincerely took advantage of this club.

Note: School prayers were taken out of schools in 1963 following a movement and lawsuit by atheist, Madalyn Murray O'Hair (1919-1995). Her case was heard in the US Supreme Court to have prayers banned in public schools across the United States. The decision in Murray v. Curlett, combined with Abington v. Schempp, ended school prayer in public schools ever since.

Of course, John said he was called the Jesus freak in school by some kids, because of his strong faith, but he didn't care; he would challenge people that didn't believe. He would quote the Holy Bible if they had doubts. For some people/students, he did feel he helped them to have a better understanding of God.

John went on to talk about his two best friends growing up, Steve and Pete, who never judged and always were supportive of each other's religious choices and beliefs because they knew they were all serving the same God. These great lifetime friends were, and still are, so dear to John's heart and I'm sure it's mutual.

As John was sharing his strong faith, he mentioned he had originally felt he should have been a priest and was planning on being a priest. His path changed when he thought God was sending him another message. I spoke up and thought it was funny that he wanted to be a priest, because for years I wanted to be a nun. We both chuckled about that for a moment. Meanwhile, it was at this point I started thinking, Is this the one God has sent me? I did pray for a religious man that loves children and would love my children as his own, then I realized I didn't want to get ahead of myself, even though I did keep my prayer to God in my mind.

MY CHILDHOOD

Now, it was my turn to share my family upbringing, which was somewhat different from his in some areas and very similar in other ways. Religion in both of our families was very important and attending church weekly was important to grow as God's loving children. Both of our families enjoyed boating, swimming, camping, and many outdoor activities.

On my father's side, there were nine children. All of my dad's siblings were extremely close throughout their lives. My grandfather came here from Poland and worked for the railroad system. My grandmother's family came over from France.

My father joined the Marines when he was in his early 20's. He was stationed in Japan and took pride in climbing Mount Fuji. In his early 20's he married my mother. When my father returned from Japan, he taught my brother and me how to eat with chopsticks. I still eat with chopsticks when I eat oriental foods. My father was, and still is, very proud of serving our country. After retiring he volunteer at the Delaware's Veterans Hospital transporting patients to and from their doctors' appointments. He is an excellent artist and did graphic arts as his career.

On my mother's side there were only two children. My mother's only sibling was a brother who was 13 years her senior. My mother told me, when she was a little girl, her brother would bring his friends over to see her. He was so proud of her, and said she was so adorable. Her brother, my Uncle Walter, was a great baseball player. My mother's father was a great golfer and had many trophies to prove it. Before he passed, he shot a hole-in-one which hit the newspapers. She was glad she could have that paper to remember his legacy in the sport.

After my brothers and I moved out of the home and on our own, my mother got a job at Cigna Healthcare Insurance. She was there until they closed their doors. She enjoyed raising us children, but she also took pride in her years working. As a mother and wife, she also took pride in her home and outside gardens. She has a green thumb, something I did not inherit. My mothers' ancestry is British and Cherokee.

Our family did almost everything with the relatives on my father's side. With a lot of aunts, uncles, and cousins, we celebrated all of our holidays together. We would take turns going to each other's houses to celebrate with food, dance and playing games.

I GIVE THIS TO YOU LORD

I am the middle child of my two brothers. Mark is my eldest brother by nearly two years and my, (as I call him) baby brother Jon, is nearly seven years my junior. It is wonderful seeing our families flourish with our nieces, nephews, and their growing families.

After sharing my story, I had the thought, Oh boy, were our daughters right. We did have a great deal in common, especially with him wanting to be a priest and I wanting to be a nun and the fact we both adore children and absolutely love our Lord and our families. We talked for hours and got to learn a lot about one another. We both still enjoy the outdoor life of boating, camping, swimming, and sharing time with our children most of all. Even though we are not a nun or a priest, we are still very strong in our faith and active in our church. John and I went to Holy Cross Catholic Church, the same church and location where our children were attending school. We went from being nervous to feeling so comfortable and engaging in deep conversations. I shared more with him than I had shared with people I'd known for years. I'm not sure why I opened up so much; I guess it just felt right.

After John and I finished our few hours of conversation we said good night and went our separate ways. I was glad I made the choice to accept his offer for coffee and dinner.

THE MESSAGE

Bible Verses of God Answering Our Prayers: *https://usccb.org*

>**Matthew 7:7** *"Ask, and it will be given to you; seek, and you will find; knock, and it will be opened to you."*

>**John 16:24** *"Until now you have not asked anything in My name; ask and you will receive, so that your joy may be complete."*

>**Psalms 145:18** *"The Lord is near to all who call upon Him, to all who call upon Him in truth."*

And there are many more verses in the Bible of the promises of Our Lord who answers our prayers. The Lord knows our future and what is best for us, so if He answers our prayers differently than we asked, we must understand it was for our own good. Sometimes we need to break the mold of where we came from before we can move forward peacefully.

CHAPTER 5

A ROMANTIC PROPOSAL

John and I began conversing on the phone, often. At times we would talk for an hour or so. Then, one day he asked me out on a "real" date. He asked if I'd be interested in going to dinner and a movie. I told him, *"I would like that very much."* and that's just what we did; it was a very nice first date. We were getting more comfortable talking to each other.

After that night John and I began dating on a regular basis. One night, John's ex-wife invited me over to her place. When I arrived, she began telling me things about John. She said he liked to dance, and he loved to sing old songs, like from the 40's. And with all she had told me; everything she said were good things about John. She and I also were acquaintances, and it was comforting to hear her tell me things about John that he probably wouldn't have told me himself. I was happy she opened up to me and we were able to share some time together. She had her place looking very nice and I especially liked the table she and the kids hand painted together. The children each put their painted handprints on the table. It was so adorable with the different colors and different hand sizes. I'm sure they had fun creating great memories doing it too.

Eventually, John and I started doing things that included all the kids. They got along exceptionally well together, and it made things much nicer.

Once, when I was at John's house, I noticed a person I recognized on a business card that was on his refrigerator. The lady was a realtor who happened to be a neighbor of mine and my ex-years prior. I asked him how he knew her and shared my connection. He said they were good friends with her and the family. I recalled a memory of a man with dark hair, dark beard and mustache playing with his children. At that moment it hit me. I surprisingly said, *"Oh my gosh, I saw you and your family at their house during their daughter's Confirmation party. You were playing with your kids."* I remembered this because of how nice it was seeing a man taking the time to play with his children. How funny! John does have a distinct look about himself, which makes it easy for people to recollect seeing him. He said they were at that party, which confirmed my thoughts. What were the odds we were at the same place at the same time before our girls ever met in school? Talk about a small world. God, being wonderful as He is, has had His eyes on us and decided to make the connection. And it was at that moment I was convinced this was the man God had sent my way. Thank you, Jesus, for answering my prayer.

  As time passed, our relationship became very serious, and we were inseparable. Because of our relationship, we both agreed it would be best if we were not working at the same place. We wanted to keep ourselves professional. Since he was the CFO, I knew it was best for me to seek new employment. And I had no problems finding another job with the help of a dear friend of mine, Margaret.

  Margaret said there was a position opened where she worked. I went for an interview and was hired fairly quickly for the position of being a Philip Morris representative. I gave my two weeks' notice at the optometrist practice before starting the new job. It was a bittersweet departure, however, they were happy for John and me, and of course completely understood our position. I think they respected us for it. I liked my job and of course seeing my dear friend Margaret was always a bonus.

I GIVE THIS TO YOU LORD

THE SET-UP

Friday, May 16th I will hold dear to my heart forever, because it's my younger brother Jon's birthday, but also because at 1:00 pm I received a call from the front desk at work asking me to come downstairs to pick up a package. This request wasn't unusual; I received deliveries all the time with new Philip Morris products. But, when I arrived at the front desk, to my surprise, the clerk handed me a long stem flower shaped box. When I opened it, I saw a beautiful single long stem red rose inside with a card that read, *"I hope you are happy today! I love you! John."* then on the back it read, *"Will?"* Well, when I went back upstairs everyone thought that was cute, but we all agreed the message on the back was a bit puzzling. Then at exactly 2:00 pm I received another call from the front desk asking me to come downstairs to pick up another package. So, I went downstairs to find another long stem flower shaped box. I took the rose shaped box upstairs before opening it. There were two beautiful long stem roses inside with a card that read, *"2 roses signifying the two of us joined in love, Love John"*, on the back it read, *"You?"* Now this is just funny, yet again the messages were cryptic. I added the two flowers into the vase I had already put my first flower in. They were vibrant red and beautiful.

My co-workers were near my phone before it rang at 3:00 pm and they were not disappointed. At exactly 3:00 pm I received the message to pick up another package at the front desk. The clerk was smiling as she handed me the box while participating in these unusually delightful moments. My co-workers insisted I wait to open it when I get back upstairs. When I opened the box there were three beautiful red long stem roses, as we all expected. A co-worker had a larger vase ready to go to support the additional new roses. The card read; *"I hope you are reading the back of these cards!"* *"Three o'clock, three roses, three words, "I love you! Love John."* And on the back it read *"Be My?"*

Now at 3:30 I had to go into my boss's office for a three-way phone conference with Philip Morris' main office, another Philip Morris office, and our office. It was relevant that I be present to read off the monthly product inventory reports for the meeting. While looking down at my watch and still in the meeting at 4:00 pm, I couldn't help but think about the possibility of another box waiting for me when I got out of the meeting. I had to admit it was difficult staying focused during this particular meeting. My mind was wondering, *Is there another box of flowers waiting for me with another cryptic message from John?* When the conference meeting ended at 4:30 pm, I came out of my boss' office to hastily reach my desk without tripping on my way. And that's when I saw it, another long-stemmed flower box sitting on my desk. My co-workers anxiously waited for me to return to my desk to open the box. With my eyes twinkling and a big smile on my face I gently opened the box. And there were my four long stem red roses. What a beautiful arrangement I had now in my rose filled vase. The card inside read, *"Now & Forever! Love, your John"*. The back read, *"Dinner Date? At 5 pm. Please call the house & leave a message yes or no. If yes, I will pick you up at CRI at 5 pm."* Myself and my co-workers laughed at the final message. I think these messages made it an exciting day for everyone. How clever and fun it was to receive all these flowers and amazing messages for a date. Of course, I said yes.

At 5:00 pm co-workers were leaving for the weekend. I was finalizing a few things for Philip Morris as requested during our meeting. When I was finished, I put on my sweater, grabbed my purse and vase full of the beautiful red roses John sent me. As I was leaving with my flowers, it made me smile just thinking about how special John made my day. I was looking forward to our dinner engagement.

As I exited the building, I could see all my co-workers cheering and clapping at the sight of a chauffeur greeting me in front of a long black limousine. The sharply dressed chauffeur came up to me and asked, *"Are you Ms. Darlene?"* I replied, *"Yes, I am."* He guided me to the door and opened it. Inside was my handsome John wearing a snazzy suit and a big smile. While I climbed into the limo, I could see dozens of absolutely gorgeous deep red roses all over the limo. I was smiling from ear to ear and gave him a big kiss once the doors closed. He asked me, *"Were you surprised?"* I said, *"Yes, I had no idea!"* I thanked him for all the beautiful roses.

Day John Proposed May 16, 1997

Once I was settled in I shared how my day played out with my co-workers and their anxiety waiting for more flowers to arrive every hour. I admitted my excitement too, especially for the phone to ring on the dot of each hour. I told him this was the first time I've ever been in a limousine and the beautiful flowers were far more than I'd ever received in a lifetime. I could see he was happy that I enjoyed his surprise. He told me not to pay attention to what's outside; he wanted to surprise me with where we were going to dinner.

Later John told me the chauffeur asked, *"How will I know which one is Ms. Darlene?"* John replied, *"She will be the one holding a bunch of flowers."*

THE DATE

We talked, joked, and kissed several times as we drove a while before arriving to our destination. When we arrived, we were in Philadelphia in front of a restaurant called *The Victor Café*. This was quite a hike from our hometown. Inside The Victor Café were waiters and waitresses that sang operatic Italian aria while guests enjoyed their meal. They were opera singers from local theaters who also worked and sang at this establishment. I'd never been exposed to anything as elaborate as this restaurant in my life. It was so sweet how John thoughtfully organized this lovely evening together. Prior to this evening, he told me he was going to surprise me every now and then with some special date nights out. It was the most romantic experience I'd ever had up to that point.

The restaurant was well-known for its authentic representation of Italy at its finest. The ambiance of the lights, the music, the murals, the waiters' uniforms, all went well throughout. I felt like we stepped into Italy, even though I'd never been there.

John and I were seated immediately, and placed our drink orders. John said he had to use the restroom and he'd be right back. As I was looking over the menu I noticed it wasn't a cheap place to eat by any means. John came back to our table and then the waiter started to sing an opera aria to us. Our waiter, to me, looked a lot like the Italian singer Pavarotti. He not only looked like him, but he also sang just like him. He was looking right into my eyes as he sang in Italian. John was translating what he was singing.

From behind the waiter's back, the waiter pulled around a medium sized vase full of miniature roses. In the vase were seven white roses and two red roses with baby's breath embellishing its beauty. The seven white miniature roses represented the unity of our seven children and the two red miniature roses represented John's and my love for one another.

Another waiter went behind our waiter as he was singing and then our waiter brought from behind his back an opened jewelry box showing a magnificent diamond ring. John's translation of the words, were, *"The beauty of the roses do not compare to your beauty"*, and *"Your eyes sparkled more than any diamond."* Then the waiter stopped singing and John got on his knees in front of me. The restaurant became so quiet you could hear a pin drop. He asked the question, *"Will you marry me?"* I was crying happy tears and said without hesitation, *"Yes, I would love to marry you!"* and we hugged and kissed. I could see he too had a little tear in his eye. It was truly a tender moment. Then an elderly woman a distance from our table yelled out, *"What did she say?"* People simultaneously said, *"She said, 'Yes!"* Then the music between the opera singers started again with another waiter walking around as they sang.

This magical proposal was planned out so perfectly, I knew he put a tremendous amount of thought into his proposal. I loved every moment and I still think of our special night often.

It was ironic that next to our table was a Catholic priest with other guests at his table. The priest came over and wished us many blessings. When people passed by our table as they were leaving, they said, *"Best Wishes"* and *"Congratulations"*. One of John's business associates sent a bottle of champagne to our table. It was one of the most beautiful proposals I've ever heard of or seen.

As if the evening wasn't perfect enough, John had pre-planned announcing our engagement to our children and our parents, if I said yes to his proposal. And I'm sure everyone we knew already knew what my answer would be. Some of my friends probably thought I was crazy for marrying a man with five children, but as I've said, I always wanted a large family. God sure does provide, in His timing. And I love every one of our seven children.

THE ANNOUNCEMENT

First, we arrived at my mom's home in New Castle, Delaware about an hour north of where we lived. When we arrived, my mother already had a table full of food to celebrate my brother Jon's birthday and our announcement with our family. I was glad to wish my brother a Happy Birthday in person.

After leaving my mother's place we got back into the limo and headed to John's parents' house. Our children were staying with them while we were on our engagement date. When we pulled up in the limo the children were running and jumping up and down in excitement as they rushed over to check out the inside of the limo. They especially *"wow-ed"* the elegant blue subtle lighting and all the beautiful roses inside. The older girls wanted to open the roofs visor to stick their heads out just to say they did it. The driver was cool about it and opened the sunroof for them.

It was fun sharing that moment with our children. It was particularly special seeing them so happy we were getting married, and knowing our two families would become one big family. John's parents were also so happy for us and our growing family. And I had to respect the fact John asked my father for his permission to marry me, despite our age. My father gave his blessings.

What a wonderful moment to share with our children and families. It was truly a magnificent, majestic night all around, and one we both will treasure forever.

CHAPTER 6
UNITY OF TWO FAMILIES

The days that followed, John and I started making critical decisions on our wedding plans. Uniting our two families was an important step that affected each one of us, so it was essential to include all seven of our children in the wedding. In a sense, we were all marrying each other and we would be connected forever. Some of our dearest friends were also in our wedding, making it a good-sized wedding party. As John and I were going through preparatory details, we carried on like a couple of kids. It was fun and exciting to plan a wedding our way, even if it wasn't an exact tradition to others.

We chose a Christmas-themed wedding since this was our absolute favorite time of the year, a time when most people demonstrate a peaceful caring manner throughout the Holy holiday season. So, to us it truly was a magical time of the year. Although it technically wasn't landing on Christmas, it was close enough to create a Christmas setting.

THE PREPARATIONS

John suggested we get married on November 22nd, because it would be the number 4 (2 + 2 = 4). I loved it and thought, *how perfect*. While corny for most, it was an important number/date for us. The number 4 had a significant meaning for John and me. It had always been John's favorite number throughout his life, even though he didn't know why. So, naturally it was special to me as well. Most people had pagers back then instead of cell phones. We used them to relay secret codes daily. John and I sent number messages back and forth to signify our love in multiple forms of 4's, ie., 444, 4444, 44444444...etc... It meant, *"I love you"*, or *"I'm thinking about you"*, or *"See you very soon"*. So naturally it only made sense for us to get married at exactly 4:44 pm.

Shortly after getting married, we discovered something incredible. John's parents were packing their belongings from their home to move into a new home. They came across something they thought would be interesting for John and me to know. So, immediately they contacted John saying, *"We need you and Darlene to come over right away."* They said it wasn't an emergency. We dropped what we were doing and went to their home immediately. What his parents found and wanted to share with us was his older deceased brother Vincent's birth certificate. When they handed it to us, we saw Vincent's time of birth. It was 4:44 pm when he entered this world. Instantly, we both got chills and believe his brother Vincent is one of his guardian angels. It explained a lot about the purpose for feeling the connection to the number 4. John feels it's Vincent's way of letting him know he is watching over him. Since being married, I've seen multiple 4's even when I'm traveling alone. I believe Vincent is also watching over me and possibly our whole family.

Before the wedding John considered a creative vehicle option for our large family. Currently, John owned a high 15 passenger van. So, instead of struggling with getting the younger children in and out by climbing up and in, then out and down from the van, he suggested a more comfortable practical solution for everyone. We both knew our lives were about to become very busy with meeting all the children's activities and needs. John had an epiphany and asked, *"What do you think about a second-hand limousine or hearse?"* I laughed and said, *"The hearse is absolutely out of the question, but I would certainly entertain the idea of a limousine!"* I had no idea how much a used limo would cost, but John's a pretty good negotiator; I had faith in him finding something for the family. We

I GIVE THIS TO YOU LORD

discussed the multiple benefits it could serve our family, such as using it for our wedding, if we could find one quickly. We could use it for the many proms and homecomings for seven children. We could fit a sports team in it, we could use it for friends' and family's weddings, and so much more with our growing family. So, once we decided this was the type of vehicle we were considering, John was fast on the task of finding one before the wedding. Meanwhile, I continued working on other wedding details.

Then, just a couple days after deciding to get a limo, John came to me and said, *"I found the perfect limousine. It's a white super stretch Lincoln limousine, perfect for the wedding, and it's affordable."* Fortunately, it was only an hour away. We dropped the kids off at John's parent's house and picked it up after having a mechanic checking it out. The mechanic said it was in great shape and a steal of a deal.

We hadn't shared our adventurous whimsical find with the children. When we arrived at John's parent's house in the limo, the kids all came out of the house; John had called ahead of our arrival to have his parents send the kids outside. It was amazing watching the surprised expressions on each of their faces, especially when John asked the kids, *"So, what do you think of our new family car?"* The kids were in awe. They didn't believe him at first, so he really had to convince them we did buy it. Their reactions were priceless. We piled the kids in the vehicle and went for a ride, then we came back for our visit with his parents who also checked it out.

The timing for the vehicle was perfect, we were able to purchase it just before the wedding and the kids loved traveling in it too. Inside there was a TV, VCR, drawers under the seats for storing movies, an ice chest for beverages, which was great for the kids when we went on trips. We had two dividers between the front and the back of the vehicle; one was a slightly tinted glass visor panel, which was excellent to see everything going on in the back. The other was a solid visor panel giving complete privacy between the two spaces. The privacy divider was a perfect feature for times when the kids were watching a movie or napping. We enjoyed being able to listen to our own type of music or to just talk to each other, while the children had their space in the back. The limo was especially fun when we'd go through a fast-food chain window. John would pay for the food at the driver's window, then pull up so the kids could retrieve their food through the back window.

Hala by Our Family Vehicle

In our first year of marriage, John and I created a new tradition for our family while they were young. Every Christmas Eve after church we'd take our children across the street to a local hospital. We'd take a large basket full of different types of nicely stuffed animals, and go straight to the children's ward, where we'd get permission at the nurse's station to allow children to pick out whichever animal they wanted. The nurses were delighted we thought of them on such an important night for children. Some children couldn't decide between a few toys so we would give them all their favorites. This tradition was important, and a time our children could reflect on how blessed they were to celebrate Christmas at home with their family. Seeing these poor children in the hospital alone on Christmas Eve was sad. It warmed our hearts to put smiles on the children's faces and to give them something new to hug to comfort them throughout their difficult night.

THE WEDDING CEREMONY

On Saturday November 22, 1997, we were married in a Methodist church in Camden, DE by John's brother-in-law, Pastor Jerry. It was a special moment and an honor to have Jerry perform our matrimonial occasion. And at exactly 4:44 pm I started walking down the aisle to join John at the altar. Prior to the wedding, we found humor in some phone calls we received from guests asking if the time on the invitation was a typo. We'd chuckle and I'd say, *"Nope, it's not a typo, it's the exact time I'll be walking down the aisle. It's just an important time for us and we wanted to incorporate it in our wedding plans."*

Once our annulments were finalized through the Catholic Church, we were re-married in our own church, Holy Cross Parish Church in Dover, Delaware. Seeing all seven of our children in the wedding was just beautiful. We had a couple of our friends and family members in the wedding too.

All Our Children in Wedding

Hala was two-and-a-half years old and the youngest of the seven, so, it seemed natural for her to be a flower girl. Stephanie would be turning 12 just four days before the wedding and she agreed to be a flower girl with Hala, which was a blessing since Stephanie was very helpful in getting Hala down the aisle without fear or complications. A dear friend of ours went to New York to purchase material to make both beautiful flower girl dresses. They were gorgeous Cinderella style full-length red dresses with a hint of white ribbon and roses. Noah was our ring bearer. He looked so dapper in his little black and white tuxedo. John III and Michael stood with their father, also quite dapper in their tuxedos. Crystal and Ashley were beautiful bridesmaids, and it was an honor to have them by my side. The ages of the children when we were married were; Hala - two-and-a-half; Noah – five-and-a-half; John – eight; Michael - 10, Stephanie - 12, Ashley - 14, and Crystal - 15. Yes, God has blessed us. All the girls looked so beautiful, and the boys looked incredibly handsome. We were proud parents having them stand with us during such an important and meaningful time for all of us. I was sure the Lord knew that in my heart I wanted this big family and I had so much love to offer them, so as we were married, John and I became the proud parents of seven wonderful children.

Our wedding was exactly as we wanted it to be, festive with colors of red, white, black and evergreen. The ladies in the wedding wore soft fluffy white hand muffs with some Christmas flowers on them. They looked perfect with their red and white festive dresses. I held a large artificial (yet realistic looking) single red rose with a very long steam. The red rose had meaning; it was how John proposed to me.

Our two flower girls in their red Cinderella-looking, perfect dresses spread rose petals on the floor just before I walked up the aisle. Hala's favorite princess was Cinderella, so John and I told her she was wearing a Cinderella Christmas dress. She was glowing as she walked down the aisle.

When I was walking down the aisle, I could see my handsome John in his black and white tuxedo. We both had big smiles on our faces and watched each other as I got closer to him. Everything was so beautiful. I'm happy I accepted that second chance date with John; it was one of the best decisions I've ever made. One the Lord laid out for both of us.

THE RECEPTION

For the reception, we bought a huge Christmas tree to place at the entrance of our festively decorated reception hall at Maple Dale Country Club in Dover, DE. Inside our invitation envelopes, instead of asking our guests to purchase and wrap a wedding gift, we asked everyone to pick out an ornament that illustrated their personality, then add their name on a tag and decorate our tree as they entered the reception hall.

When guests arrived, they enjoyed decorating the large Christmas tree. Guests were great about handwriting their names on a tag attached to the ornaments, and some of the ornaments certainly exemplified their personalities. We love each one of our ornaments. These were gifts we knew we would treasure forever. Today we have enough ornaments to dress three Christmas trees, and sometimes we do. For our centerpieces we selected miniature trees with white Christmas lights already lit for guests as they arrived to be seated. Next to each tree was a gift box. Inside the gift box were miniature decorations and garland for guests to decorate their centerpiece trees on the tables. Many guests said they loved decorating the trees. This was something guests got to do while waiting for us to finalize pictures at the church and beeping the limousine's horn around town on our way to the reception. They also enjoyed wine, cheese, crackers, dips, and fresh fruit until we arrived. Our professionally decorated cake was absolutely stunning and tasty. Of course, since we were doing the wedding our way, we decided to make the cake a little more interesting. We chose two tiers of the cake to be banana flavored, (one was our top cake layer), and the other layers individually were strawberry, peach and chocolate; a flavor for everyone to choose and enjoy.

The entertainment we selected was a married couple we met at a wedding expo. Their entertainment title was called, *The Best of Both Worlds.* She was a fabulous singer, and he was an awesome DJ. The couple was so cute together and certainly complimented each other.

She wore an elegant gold and black formal sequined gown. He was sporting a sleek black and white tuxedo to perform his DJ magic. When she sang, she walked around the room using her amazing God given voice. She sounded exactly like the artist whose song she sang. Her powerful voice could range from songs by Whitney Houston and Bette Midler to other famous female musical artist. They were a classy couple and a perfect fit for our dream wedding.

John and I danced to our song, "I Finally Found Someone©, by Barbara Streisand and Brian Adams. So true, we did finally find someone—the one. We, along with many of our guest danced a lot. Complications later in life would make me cling to these precious memories.

Wedding November 22, 1997

Everyone appeared to enjoy seeing all the family together. The photographer captured some nice family and friends group pictures. We were happy to see so many family members attending the wedding. The children also enjoyed dancing with their cousins. We invited family from all over the country. Usually when you send out invitations you don't expect everyone to attend, so not only did all 250 guests attend, but we also had a few attendees ask to bring extra guests. It was so wonderful; they all traveled a great distance to witness our special day. We loved seeing all our relatives, friends, and co-workers collectively having a great time. It was the beginning of a new and amazing life together.

THE HONEYMOON

After going to each table and thanking family and friends for coming and traveling so far to witness our special day, we were off on our honeymoon in Florida. We spent several days enjoying all of Disney Worlds theme parks, went to a mystery dinner theater, enjoyed live shows, toured Alligator Land, enjoyed the *"Ripley's Believe It or Not"* museum and much more. We also found our way out of a human maze after successfully completing trivia clues throughout the maze. For me, this was really a treat, as I had never been this far away from home in my lifetime. So, Disney World was a dream come true for me.

Our honeymoon extended into the Thanksgiving holiday. Our dinner was in a magnificent romantic restaurant that served every delicious, home-cooked, typical Thanksgiving food we normally would have enjoyed at home. It was a perfect Thanksgiving for our first Thanksgiving dinner as a married couple. As lovely and romantic as it was, we both admitted it wasn't the same without all our children.

We love having them with us for Thanksgiving, because we are thankful to have them in our lives. Now, Thanksgiving is a tradition for all our children and their families to come to our house. During our Thanksgiving celebration we also exchange Christmas gifts. What great times we have and wonderful memories we build together while watching our family grow in numbers.

Our honeymoon also included Black Friday, and boy, did we do some shopping. We went crazy and bought so many Christmas gifts for the kids, we had to buy more luggage to bring it all home on the flight. It was the honeymoon I'd always dreamt of having; playful, romantic, peaceful, and with my best friend, lifetime partner and soulmate.

Now that the honeymoon was over, our lives were about to get busy—real busy. It takes two strong parents to be physically up for the challenge of raising seven different personalities. We were geared up and ready for the quest, but life doesn't always go as planned.

CHAPTER 7

MY BLESSED LIFE RATTLED WITH ILLNESS

After the honeymoon we had to get ourselves into an organized routine for a family with seven children. First, we considered all the children's extracurricular activities; where they were located, what time they started and ended, and then we decided who was going to take whom to what activities. Most times John and I had to go in opposite directions to meet all the demands efficiently. I'm sure this type of schedule would drive some people crazy, but we loved having a big family. We had a lot of energy, and enjoyed all the challenges that came with it. Of course, as the children got older, their schedules changed and so did our routine.

CREATING A ROUTINE

Between all the sports, play practice and plays, musical concerts, award ceremonies, sleepovers, birthday parties, parades, dances, homecomings, proms, and much more, kept us busy. It took the two of us to meet all of the demands needed to function smoothly as a large family. When I became ill, it had a tremendous effect on our lives.

Despite our crazy schedules, we made one-on-one time every day for each of our children, even if it was to play a simple game, listen to their day's events, listen to a new song they liked, help them with a project, or whatever was going on in their lives. We felt it was important to give them structure for a healthy transition to grow into the demographics of our big family. As far as helping the kids with homework, I took on the science and English subjects and John took on all the math, since numbers were more his thing than mine. We both shared helping with history and I was the creative one to help with school projects in all subjects.

Every Sunday afternoon, we had Family Movie Night with the kids. This was our fun family time to snuggle up with the kids while eating popcorn and drinking soda. Good times and good memories.

After getting home from work, while the children were doing their homework, I'd start dinner and John loved helping in the kitchen. Now, he cooks all the time. He's a far better cook than I. His mother and grandmother taught him and his siblings all they know. Now, he enjoys creating his own new delicious meals. I'm quite the baker and he's an amazing cook, so it works well for us.

When our family went to church, the children were such angels. A few times we had people ask, *"How do you keep your kids so calm?"* We would respond by shrugging our shoulders saying, *"It's how they are, all the credit goes to them."* They were happy children and well mannered. We were blessed. Don't get me wrong, when they hit the teen years there were a few that went through that awkward *"I know everything"* stage. Isn't that a fun time with children? Seriously, when they get through that stage it's downhill from there.

FAMILY TRIP

We started a tradition of taking family trips to Orlando, Florida every two years. There was always at least one adventure to reminisce about. One time we went on vacation with my mother and another family member to our time-share called, *"Westgate Resorts"*, which is only three miles from Disney World. We all traveled together in our stretch limousine. That made 11 people, and it was still a comfortable ride. On this particular trip, Hala

I GIVE THIS TO YOU LORD

was four-and-a-half years old, and the only child using a car seat. Whenever we traveled great distances, we preferred to travel systematically at night. It was the perfect time to travel with children because most children slept through the trip. This means we had fewer bathroom breaks, we didn't have to worry about hungry bellies for hours, and it was quiet for half the trip. They liked it too, because when they'd wake up, it seemed like they were getting a lot closer to our vacation destination.

On this particular trip we were scarcely gone an hour before a 12-point buck (huge deer) took an enormous leap from the center island of trees along the road into the hood of our limo. John, John III (his dad's navigator), and Noah were all in the front seat when this ill-fated accident occurred. The deer struck our vehicle at approximately 1:00 am, shortly after Noah had fallen asleep. The enormous hood of our flawless Lincoln flipped open when this massive deer landed and rolled off onto the ground next to where John pulled over. The other eight of us in the back were barely aware of what had just happened. Lincolns are great solid cars; another good reason to own one. We hardly felt a thing, except some of our belongings shifting from the back window and onto Ashley's head. It wasn't serious, but enough to be uncomfortable for her.

With the privacy visor up between us, I was unable to see what had happened and quickly asked John, *"Are you guys ok?"* and John said at the same time, *"We just hit a deer; we're fine. How is everyone back there?"* John got out of the limo to check on us as he was relieved to see we were all ok. Thank God we were all fine. Hala was still sleeping and never knew a thing.

Fortunately, we had cell phones by then. John brought two cell phones with him, and I had my phone with me. The three cell phones were all needed and used. John was able to contact our insurance agency to report the accident, he contacted the police to report the accident, then he contacted AAA, then his parents. We were glad he had three cell phones because when one died, there was another one to use. We were in the middle of nowhere. John gave AAA our mile marker location and details of our situation, including how many people we had and how much luggage we had for our Florida trip. He let them know we were in a limousine.

John requested AAA to set up transportation for us when we arrived at the Baltimore Airport. He requested a 15-passenger van, and they said no problem, a van would be waiting for us at BWI when we arrived. They also said they were sending someone out to pick up all of us soon. After John's conversation with AAA, he called his parents to come and wait with our limo until it was towed away. They were relieved to know everyone was fine.

When the police officer arrived, he took one look at the 12-point buck and said in a very southern drawl, *"That's the biggest deer I've ever seen, can I have 'im?"* John and I were surprised, and John said, *"Sure, help yourself!"* To this day we still laugh about how he asked for the deer. Before leaving us, the officer said he would have someone travel the road every now and then to make sure we were ok. We appreciated his gesture and thanked him. He was very nice. The police did check on us every now and then, which I'm sure made John feel safer.

Nearly two hours went by before John gave AAA another call. They should have been at our location by this time. When the guy answered, John asked, *"How close are you?"* He insinuated they were having trouble finding us. The guys asked, *"How will I find you?"* John gave the man the mile marker again and said, *"I'm pretty sure we are the only stretch limousine on the side of the road."* All of us in the back could hear his conversation and those of us still awake chuckled.

Another hour went by before they finally arrived. We were so thankful Hala slept through the whole thing. In fact, she never woke up until we arrived at the airport, including transferring her from the limo and into the AAA vehicle, which was not an easy task. We put everyone in the vehicles first, then added her last so we didn't disturb her. Hala's a sound sleeper.

To our amazement AAA sent us two very small Chevy Cavaliers. Mind you, we had 11 people and each of these little cars only had four seats, including the drivers. Not to mention we had a suitcase for each one of us, a few extra bags, pillows, and blankets. Plus, my mother had baked an anniversary cake for John and me.

So, thank goodness my husband is the best packer in the world. He succeeded in packing each car as tightly as he could, and we barely made it, but with his magical physics skills he managed to make it happen. He placed all flat items across the seats, such as blankets, pillows, jackets, and anything else flat. On top of these mounds, he scrunched as many of us as he could across each seat, including three across one of the back seats. First the adults, then the older children. On top of them were the younger children, and on top of the younger children were lighter bags. The trunks of both vehicles were packed tight. So, in one of these tiny vehicles he managed to get six of us in, not including the driver. In the other vehicle there were five, not including the driver. Hala's car seat took up a whole spot making the challenge even more difficult. We were amazed by how Hala slept through all this commotion. Boy, her angels must have been protecting her or maybe she was dreaming of being at Disney World? When Hala woke up, she was surprised we weren't in the limo. We still laugh about how sound she slept that night.

It was 4:00 am when they rescued us, about three hours after we called. It took about half an hour to unload and strategically load the two vehicles. When we reached the Baltimore Airport, John went directly to get our van that was supposedly waiting for us. Apparently, they said it was going to take a couple hours, because AAA didn't reserve a van for us. John wasn't happy; we were promised a vehicle, and he knew his family was tired and hungry. While at the airport we picked at the cake my mom made for our anniversary. Thank goodness we had it to nibble on.

When John came back, he told us he wanted all of us to sit with our luggage in the center of the airport. It had already been a very long night/morning. The kids understood our predicament and were patient through it all, thank goodness. We didn't like parking ourselves in the center of things, but we needed a vehicle sooner than much later. Airports weren't as crowded then as they are these days. We presume they wanted to get us out of the way too, because it wasn't long before they had a 15-passenger van ready for our family. Hallelujah!

Once we all piled into the van, John was pumped up for the long trip. First thing we did was stop to satisfy everybody's stomachs. Then, most of us—including me—fell asleep after our lost sleep from the night before. Once we crossed the Georgia line, Hala started getting sick in the van just behind the driver's seat. Thank goodness there was a shoulder, and John immediately pulled over. Everyone jumped out because of the wretched stench of vomit. The kids were making gagging sounds as they were quickly rushing out of the van. John started cleaning the van and I started tending to Hala to get her out of the car seat, stripping her down and cleaning her up with baby wipes and fresh clothes.

While the kids and my mother were outside the van, a massive boar came out from the trees near the roadside and was heading in our direction, that was, until all the girls freaked out and started screaming and laughing as they tried to push each other to hurriedly get back into the van despite the smell. They had never seen a boar in person, and I think the boar had never seen screaming girls before, because that boar jumped up on all fours, turned around, and ran back into the woods. It looked like a scene from the Jurassic Park movie, with bushes swaying back and forth while the animal made its way back into the woods. He was a big one.

Funny thing was, before the trip we prayed for a great trip and told the kids, *"Let's go make some new memories!"* God sure does have a good sense of humor, because the kids clearly do have memories from this adventurous trip. The kids also have a good sense of humor, because on Christmas of that year, the kids gave their dad a 12-point buck ornament to hang on our Christmas tree. And we've been hanging it on the tree every year since.

During our trip, we pre-arranged a surprise birthday party for Stephanie who was turning 13 during our vacation. So, while we were enjoying a day at the Disney World parks, the resort was decorating for Stephanie's party and setting up the food we had delivered. We gave specific instructions, and it went off perfectly for her. We told the kids we wanted to go back to the resort for lunch and to let the little ones take a short nap, then we could go back to Disney World for the rest of the day. All the kids except Stephanie knew about the party, so the kids didn't give us any trouble breaking for lunch. When we arrived back at the resort Stephanie was surprised with pretty Disney character balloons, pizzas, place settings for everyone, and a large cookie cake in the center of the huge round table. John had already set out her gifts from the kids and us before we left. He pretended he had to go back into our place for his wallet before we left early that morning. It was nice to see she was excited, happy, and surprised. Turning 13 is a big deal, and I'm glad it worked out the way it did. The children had a great time at the lunch birthday celebration. After the party, everyone was ready to head back to one of their favorite places in the world. Hala did get her nap in the stroller when we got back to the park. Noah was tired but pushed through the day fine.

During this vacation we went to a dinner theater called, *"Wild Bills."* We met up with our Florida friends, Beth, and Martin and their two boys. It was such a great, first-time, western experience for all of us. While eating at this dinner theater, a cowboy took center stage and performed an amazing show of tricks with his lariat. He was very talented! Then he asked for a volunteer from the audience to assist in one of his stunts. Of course, the kids pointed to their dad. Well, I'm guess all those fingers pointing to John captured the entertainer's attention, because John was called up.

On stage John had to stand perfectly still on a wall of balloons while the cowboy used knives to pop the balloons, including one between his legs. The cowboy told John to stay perfectly still, and immediately John responded with a quivering voice, *"Oh don't worry, I won't move."* The audience laughed and the kids had fun watching their dad entertain the crowd. The other half of the show exhibited traditional Native Americans wearing beautifully colored ceremonial garments to dance and tell a peaceful story of nature. It was such a spectacular meaningful experience to witness their talents. Everyone left with an appreciation for our Creator's beautiful natural gifts we sometimes take for granted.

Considering our rough trip to Florida, everything from the time we reached the resort was smooth and full of pleasurable new memories and family fun.

For years I was able to enjoy our family with all our activities, like vacations, swimming in the pool, running around and playing kickball in our yard, and other family fun. I also enjoyed being present at all the children's countless activities. I even traveled twice to Montreal Canada for field trips with John III and Noah in different years. I treasured having one-on-one time with the boys during those trips.

THE FLIP OF A SWITCH

Life was so wonderful, until this horrible 24/7 pain caused so much disorder in our lives. It was like the flip of a switch; I knew I was a great mom and wife then, like being in a nightmare, I was stripped of fulfilling those roles. It was awful watching helplessly as John was forced to juggle wearing all hats to raise seven children mostly on his own, as well as taking care of my medical and physical needs.

Once my entire being was taken over by pain, our every-other-year timeshare was more difficult for John than he'd ever admit. This wonderful man, my husband and best friend never left my side. When we went to Disney World he insisted on pushing me in a wheelchair. I wanted him to get an electric wheelchair because of the uneven grounds, but he insisted on pushing me himself. Sometimes our son John would take over to help his father. I felt so helpless and a burden, however not one time did my husband, or children make me feel that way. It's just something an ill person feels when they are dependent on others to survive, especially for simple tasks that make an ill person feel like an invalid.

THE BEGINNING

John was a member of the Elks. When we married, I joined the Elks Lodge in Dover, DE. John worked his way up to the position of Exalted Ruler, which is similar to being the president of a club after going through all positions and channels to get there.

Meanwhile, I was actively involved in the youth programs. I headed up and ran a community Hands-On Science Expo for five years. This brought in about 600 or so families from the community each year, which was great for the Elks and the exhibitors. I wrote letters every year to all our county schools to get them engaged with their students of all ages. I also wrote letters to nearly every museum from the state of Delaware, as well as business owners seeking donations for winners of our free ticket raffles. We'd pick 10 winning tickets each hour of the event, so, 40 gifts were donated per event. All prizes were educational and associated with science of all kinds. A local business donated six DVD players each year, and those went to the school with the most participating students. It took a full year to organize and plan a project of this magnitude.

Some exhibitors included various museums with hands on displays throughout Delaware, a forensic lab vehicle displaying forensic demonstrations, police officers presented the annotation software to show age progression to identify missing people, and outside I scheduled police officers to conduct K-9 attack demonstrations. Native American tribes danced a ceremonial nature story and displayed handmade tools. The Natural Resources Plantation had hands-on projects, the University of Delaware's dieticians shared healthy food with samples and guides to staying healthy, Dover ILC NASA space programs brought a spacesuit, moon rocks, photos and other space related items, the 4-H Club had activities to participate in, and a dentistry exhibit allowed people to properly brush their teeth, and everyone received their own toothbrush. I even targeted science teachers from participating schools to get their students engaging in weather experiments, electronics, computer technology, musical instruments, live reptiles, and so much more.

DARLENE M. LINK

My passion lies in the science field and, as I've said, children will always be dear to my heart. Combining my two loves, I wanted to create this massive event for children to explore the sciences with their families. And there's no better way for kids to learn science than to do it hands-on. I also created the event in hopes of influencing some children to seek careers in the science field.

Other projects I was involved in through the youth program were the *"Hoop Shoot"* (basketball event), community fishing tournaments, best decorated bike, scholarships for students attending college, and much more. One year I won the national award for Best Elks Youth Program Leader at a Missouri Elks banquet. While there, I received my award on stage in front of thousands of Elk members from all over the US. I was also named Elk of the Year from our own Elks Lodge. I mention all this to share how active my body was to handle a big family, a massive community project, and many other activities at the lodge, as well as the countless activities going on in our families lives.

My heart condition was pretty much under control through the medications I was taking, and I knew when it was time to slow down.

In my last year of the Hands-on Science Expo, I started having joint and muscle discomfort. In my last few months of this project, I started developing pain that continued to grow more severe, until it became overwhelming. I scarcely made it through my fifth year, and I knew I couldn't go on another year feeling as I did. Something was happening with my health. I knew the community would miss the family science expo, but I was forced to surrender my involvement in leading this event, as well as the other youth programs at the lodge. It was labor intensive, but a labor I loved doing. Many of the exhibitors and schools I'm sure missed participating in it as well. Their involvement gave them recognition and helped grow their businesses and museums. Unfortunately, there wasn't another person in the lodge that shared my passion for the science expo project and the many daunting hours of coordinating the abundance of responsibilities needed to keep this event alive. It was sad to give it up, and especially heartbreaking to take it away from the many schools, museums, children, and families that looked forward to it. Even our own children enjoyed volunteering for the event and missed it when it was gone.

IT WASN'T MY TIME TO GO

Here's a powerful experience John and I had one pleasant evening at the Lodge. John's ex and my ex-spouse had the children on the same weekends, every other weekend. During the weekends without the children, we enjoyed going to the lodge to socialize and just have fun together. One evening, before my body started having health concerns, really stands out for us.

John and I were enjoying friends while listening to music from an old jukebox. The dance floor was open, and John asked me if I wanted to dance to a song we consider to be our song, *I Finally Found Someone*©. We often sang this song on karaoke night. So, when he asked me, I naturally said, *"Ok"*, then got up as he escorted me to the dance floor, which was only about 10' from where we sat. When we reached the dance floor and got into position, the large *"tube"* TV above my head where I was sitting only seconds ago, came crashing down—glass front first—directly on my seat. The enormous crashing, glass breaking sound was horrifying. It made everyone jump. People gasped in shock, and some even screamed out loud in fear of what they just witnessed. If John hadn't asked me to dance, and had I not accepted, there is no doubt I wouldn't be here today. This enormous old TV was very heavy. I'm glad I said yes. Everyone was flabbergasted at how *"lucky"* I was, but to John and I know it was 0% luck and 100% blessing. I'm sure it was the intervention of an angel that put our song on the jukebox at that exact time to save my life. Needless to say, the lodge was extremely apologetic and embarrassed. The TV had been on that same shelf for years. All John and I knew was, "*it just wasn't my time to go*" Nobody knows their time, nor should they.

Some teachings in the Bible regarding this. *https://bible.usccb.org*

> **Psalms 90:12** – *Teach us to count alright, that we may gain wisdom of heart.*
>
> **Proverbs 16:9** – *The human heart plans the way: but the LORD directs the steps.*
>
> **Jeremiah 29:11** – *for the prophecy lies to you in My name; I did not send them-oracle of the LORD.*
>
> **James 4:14** – *you have no idea what your life will be like tomorrow. You are a puff of smoke that appears briefly and then disappears.*
>
> **Proverbs 16:3** – *Entrust your works to the Lord, and your plans will succeed.*

Over a couple months, my health continued to worsen. I didn't understand what was happening to my body so quickly. I started to avoid things I so loved doing. The lodge was a great getaway for us, until I became sick, and we eventually stopped going completely. With me not being able to do my duties of being a mom and wife from this illness, John was overwhelmed and exhausted with responsibilities. All the things I was able to do with the children as described in this chapter were almost completely absent from my life when my illness took full control of my body. I knew I had to seek help for this pain. I called my doctor's office and made my first appointment.

CHAPTER 8

UNUSUAL WARNING

Before the end of my science expo project and before the start of all this pain, something unusual occurred. Here's when it all started.

It was an early, beautiful, sunny morning when families were excitedly awaiting the May Day's event. With little time to spare, last minute people were crossing the streets from one side to the other, trying to squeeze in for a peek of the Dover's annual parade. Our family always arrived fairly early with blankets to spread out on our usual curbside spot. It was important to get there early when you had a big family and a favorite spot to make sure the little ones could see the parade clearly. We kicked the day off by supporting the men's buffet breakfast at the Wesley United Methodist Church, just prior to the parade. Every year a good number of dedicated men from their congregation make breakfast for the community at an affordable price. It's an all you can eat breakfast, offering pancakes, scrambled eggs, sausage, OJ and coffee. John started supporting the cause when they first presented it many years ago and he has kept this tradition with the family every year since. This feast was a favorite with our children, us adults, as well as many other families, including some of our dearest friends. The ladies in the congregation baked mouthwatering homemade goodies to sell. We'd pick up a few of the homemade delicious cookies and chewy brownies before leaving the building. This was a day to just have a good time and contribute where we could. We rarely gave the kids too many sweets, but for us, this occasion was important to keeping the tradition of supporting others.

Starting off the morning with full bellies seemed to satisfy all the children as they anxiously awaited the parade to begin. Having a large family generally meant we were most likely going to have at least one child in the parade each year. This particular year it was our youngest son Noah who played the trumpet for his Holy Cross Elementary School band.

You could feel the excitement on the streets growing. Children became antsy as they waited as patiently as they could to wave at their siblings or friends in the parade. Even though we could hear the music in the distance, we knew it would be at our feet very soon.

Then, as all seemed normal, there were two mysterious women, each having long dark hair and wearing long black coats with dark clothing on a hot sunny day. They were probably in their late 40's to early 50's. I distinctly recall them walking slowly in the direct path the parade would soon be going. Most people were pretty settled, which was why these two ladies stood out. As they slowly strolled down the street, they were looking down at people periodically, almost as if they were studying them.

To my surprise, one of these women turned to look down directly at me and said, **"You're going to have problems with your hips."** She didn't stop or miss a step as they both continued down the street. John saw them too; he and I looked at each other and said, *"That was weird."* Then we tended to our children as normal. Shortly after the stranger's message, the parade began. Our son did amazingly well, as we knew he would.

Once our tired children were settled in bed that night, John and I headed to our bed as well. I mentioned to John how odd it was for that woman to make such a statement directed towards me. *"It was kind of eerie,"* I told him. He agreed it was a little strange. Then, in no time at all, our exhausted bodies were fast asleep and we had forgotten that peculiar incident, for then.

CHAPTER 9

MY DEBILITATING DISEASE REVEALED

About a year later I started developing pain in my muscles and my joints, especially my hips. It was hard standing up sometimes. At the time I had been doing a lot of physical work with the house, my job, and keeping up with the balance of being a mom, Nonna (grandma in Italian from our two eldest daughters Crystal and Ashley), wife and lover, homemaker, cook, teacher, chauffeur, and all the other normal duties of having a big family. All this while, I was running the huge community Hands-On Science Expo. At first, I thought; *"Maybe I'm just overdoing it and need to slow down a pace or two."*

Granted, even though we still had five children living at home when the disease attacked me, it was far from easy to slow down. We always had something going on with our active family schedule.

THE DECLINE

Through all our active responsibilities, my mornings kicked off with pain in my heels. When the pressure of my feet hit the floor, pain radiated up my legs; my lower back was so stiff and painful I needed to stretch daily to loosen it up. My back would crack loudly, more than it had in the past. The pain was making it harder to function as quickly as I normally did. I recall thinking about some commercials I'd seen for older people having stiff joints and pain. I was feeling and acting older than my age. As it increased, the pain forced me to volunteer less and less. I was pushing my body so hard through the pain with the Science Expo that I was relieved when it was over, because the pain had spread throughout my joints, making it difficult to fully appreciate the event. After five years of leading the Science Expo, it just became another chapter in my life.

Some mornings when I'd get out of bed the pain was so incapacitating, I can recall thinking; *Oh my gosh, if I'm hurting this much now, I'd hate to see how I'm going to feel when I get older.* I was still in denial that something serious was wrong with me other than overdoing things, but as the days passed, more often than not, severe pain and stiffness racked my body. Because of the consistent growing pain, I was forced to let some of the simpler things go unattended, which was difficult for my organized personality. As difficult as it was, I knew I had no other options.

After a couple months of complications due to my aching joints, swelling, and muscle discomfort, I thought maybe I had Lyme's Disease. Although I didn't remember pulling a deer tick off me, or seeing a red mark indicating I had been bitten by a tick, I was merely fishing for conceivable answers to what was happening to my body. The pain increased rapidly, and I was having more difficulties functioning day-to-day. Then I started experiencing smaller joint pain too. One of my coworkers from the law firm where I worked shared her father's Lyme's Disease symptoms, and based on the similarities of his symptoms and mine, I was almost convinced I had the same thing. I thought it was worth going to the doctors to get tested.

John kept pleading with me, *"Honey, you really need to see a doctor to find out what's going on with you."* I knew he was right; it was time to make an appointment to see my family practitioner. As always, John and I had a habit of taking care of everyone but ourselves. We pushed our bodies so hard we just figured we'd get over it, or it would pass. We were too busy and stubborn to take care of our own problems, but this was getting too big for me to ignore.

After the examination with my family doctor and sharing my concerns, he decided to order a complete blood workup on me. I asked him, *"Is it possible I could have Lyme's Disease?"* The doctor replied, *"I don't think it's Lyme's, but I will order blood tests to rule it out."*

Because the pain was becoming increasingly worse, the couple weeks leading to my next appointment felt like an eternity. At my follow-up appointment, the test results came back with a significant *"D Deficiency."* That was it? I could tell the doctor was expecting results to diagnose my situation, but instead he was dumbfounded, because of the level of pain I was experiencing. Now he needed to find another possible solution. Then he thought it was possible I could have arthritis. He ordered x-rays, prescribed pain medication, and hoped I would have some relief in the four weeks before my next appointment.

Again, waiting four weeks felt like an eternity. Unfortunately, the pain was getting worse and now I was feeling fatigue during the day and had difficulty sleeping at night. This insomnia was making life so difficult for me to function during the day. I was drinking more coffee than usual at work to keep up. My muscles were aching, even to the touch. When I saw my doctor for my follow up appointment, I expressed these new complications, and I told him the medication was not working enough to relieve the horrible pain I was experiencing. My x-rays did show I had degenerative disc disease in my neck, and my lower back showed mild signs of arthritis.

My doctor had done all he could for me, therefore, referred me to a local rheumatologist who was supposed to be the best in his field. My doctor wished me well and said he would be keeping track of the rheumatologist's finding.

A NEW DOCTOR

The rheumatologist's appointment took several weeks, due to the high demand of his expertise, and the fact that all first time appointments were at least an hour long. I knew the doctor would be conducting a full examination, as well as gathering my family's medical history, current medications I was taking, and previous medical reports from my primary doctor. I was completely prepared for my appointment with a list of concerns, questions, and current medication list.

I was pleased to see the doctor had a good bedside manner. He was sympathetic and seemed thorough with the examination. During the exam he started pushing on certain points of my body and moving my limbs in various directions to grasp where my most tender and problematic points were located. I was completely honest in how it felt in all areas, by grading my pain level with the 1 to 10 scale, (10 being the worst). I was trying to stay hopeful for the resolution of getting rid of the daunting pain.

Every appointment from this one forward I had to fill out a two-sided, head-to-toe body chart. This was for patients to mark trouble areas at the time of the visit. In addition, patients had to give their current pain level by using the 1 to 10 scale. Through the months and years of seeing this doctor, my chart showed widespread marks pinpointing all the multiple troubled areas where I was experiencing pain. It scared me when I'd look at the chart during each visit; the markings were increasing and I still didn't have a diagnosis.

Before leaving my first appointment, the doctor said, *"I'd like to run a few tests on you."* I agreed and was pleased he was actively seeking answers for me by ordering more x-rays and blood work. I knew the doctor wouldn't have an answer that day, but I was confident he would have a clear diagnosis soon. He prescribed a new pain medication, and said he wanted to see me in a month.

On my way home from my appointment, I stopped by the pharmacy to drop off my new medication script. Early the following morning I went to the hospital for the necessary blood tests. I had to fast for this bloodwork. While there, I set up an appointment for my x-rays. This problem was a mystery to me and the doctors. I wanted answers sooner than later and I knew John was also anxious to find out why I was suffering from chronic pain.

John and the kids had to pick up the slack on things I normally did. I began feeling depressed and felt guilty and sad to ask them for help. I was heartbroken; I knew how active I had been, and how I could do these things without any challenges. Now, it was as if someone took "me" and replaced her with someone I didn't recognize. Not once did my family make me feel I was an imposition on them. They were wonderful in every way. They told me they understood and graciously took over in areas where I could not function. Still, I felt bad for the children and for John. I know it's a normal reaction for anyone ill and dependent on others, especially when they were once an active independent person who had normally felt the need to help others.

Through time, John had become the mom, and the dad. Prior to my illness, I was one of those people who didn't require much sleep. I could go a full night or two without sleep and function chipper and fine during the days. I'd always had insomnia due to an overactive mind, but this was different; I couldn't keep my eyes open during the day, and at night the pain and medication prevented me from getting decent restful sleep.

Often I'd think and remember hearing the words of the woman at the parade reverberating in my head, "*You're going to have problems with your hips*." It was like hearing those words just yesterday. I wasn't sure how she knew, but the bottom line is, she was correct.

FINALLY, THE DIAGNOSIS

When I arrived at my appointment, I filled out the same pain body chart. I knew its purpose was to help the doctor locate where the pain was centralized (*in my case it was broadly spread*) and the level of discomfort. I'm sure the charts saved the doctor a couple initial questions before seeing the patient.

When he did enter the examination room, he listened intently to hear what had been happening to me since my last visit. He wasn't surprised when I shared new adverse developments going on with my body, like foggy memory, and problems with my digestion. He told me the tests were negative for the things he was testing me for. He added, he believed I had acute fibromyalgia, which was something I was not familiar with, even though I had heard many females suffered from this same condition. I just wasn't aware of what type of illness it was at the time. He gave me a pamphlet on fibromyalgia and when I got home, I read it, then researched the condition further on the internet. I wanted to educate myself more on the matter.

University of Rochester Medical Center website:
https://www.urmc.rochester.edu/encyclopedia/content?ContentTypeID=85&ContentID=Poo913
WHAT IS FIBROMYALGIA?

> *Fibromyalgia is a condition that causes pain in muscles and soft tissues all over the body. It is an ongoing (chronic) condition. It can affect your neck, shoulders, back, chest, hips, buttocks, arms, and legs. The pain may be worse in the morning and evening. Sometimes, the pain may last all day long. The pain may get worse with activity, cold or damp weather, anxiety, and stress. This condition is more often diagnosed in people between the ages of 20 and 50. It is most common in middle-aged women.*

I began seeing the doctor regularly while he experimented with different pain medications to try to control the level of pain I was suffering. I still couldn't even put my foot down on the floor without pain in my heels that spread up my legs. My bones and joints were swollen and painful. My back was cracking more, and my ribs hurt as well.

In one of my visits, I burst into tears. I began crying and nearly pleading with him to find out what was happening to me. I told him, *"I can't pick up my grandchildren. I can't even hold them."* I told him as I sobbed deeply. The very concerned and sympathetic doctor said he wanted to test me for another illness called, ankylosing spondylitis. While taking notes, he began questioning me about other family members. He asked if I knew of any of my relatives who suffered with extreme joint pain. I quickly responded, *"Yes, my aunt had suffered for years, as well as her daughter and an uncle of mine. I never thought twice, because they were older than me and I attributed their pain to old age and possible arthritis issues."* The doctor said the disease he was going to test me for was a genetic disease. So, he ordered the blood test, even though in those days they thought it was mostly males afflicted with this disease. Now they believe more females had it, but were miss diagnosed.

Before leaving my appointment, the doctor prescribed medication to help my depression. My life had been turned upside down. I was coping with going from a very active person to an almost sedentary person in excruciating pain day in and day out.

I had my blood work done the next day, and two weeks later I arrived early at my doctor's office, anxious to find out what the test revealed.

When my doctor entered the room, it was finally confirmed: I had the human leukocyte antigen HLA-B27, meaning; I had ankylosing spondylitis. Getting the correct diagnosis was the first step in treating the problem in hopes for a better life. I could tell the doctor was relieved to have validation of my disease. Now, he could prescribed proper medications to treat it. He really was trying to get my body to move and function at a level I could tolerate.

WebMD defines the disease as:

> ***ANKYLOSING SPONDYLITIS, (AS) is a rare type of arthritis that causes pain and stiffness in your spine. This lifelong condition usually starts in your lower back. But it also can spread up to your neck or damage joints in other parts of your body.***
>
> ***"Ankylosis" means fused bones or other hard tissue. "Spondylitis" means inflammation in your spinal bones, or vertebrae. Severe cases can leave your spine hunched. A.S. isn't curable. But medication and exercise can ease your pain and help keep your back strong.***

Some symptoms of ankylosing spondylitis often start in the sacroiliac joints, where your spine connects to your pelvis. The signs most commonly appear before age 45.
- *Mild aches in your low back or buttocks that come and go*
- *Pain that's worse in the morning or after sitting for a long time*
- *Inflexible spine that curves forward*
- *Pain and stiffness in your shoulders, hips, hands, thighs, or even the Achilles tendon in your heel*
- *Tiredness*
- *Swelling in your joints*

Who gets Ankylosing Spondylitis? AS affects about 1% of the U.S. population, or an estimated 3.2 million people.
https://www.webmd.com/ankylosing-spondylitis/default.htm

This explains why it was so hard for the doctors to diagnose me, and the fact that it originally was believed to affect mostly men. I was so thankful there was a real diagnosis for my misery. I've learned AS is a permanent disease that lives inside the body. I'm so blessed and thankful for God's healing.

A TREATMENT PLAN

I was taking non-steroidal anti-inflammatory drugs, or NSAIDs, to help relieve some of the pain. I did recall an illness I had many years back that lasted for several months, and it was within the typical age range of the disease. I saw two doctors who couldn't figure out what was causing the pain I suffered, but after several months it was gone. It didn't hit me until I learned more about AS and how it can come and go. If that was what was happening to me years prior, it must have gone into dormancy until resurfacing again when I was nearly 50 years old. I did share my diagnosis with my relatives, and suggested they also get tested and get on a pain treatment program. It's unfortunate my aunt had passed away several years before my diagnosis. I wish her doctor had diagnosed it for her. Maybe she wouldn't have suffered as much as she did over the years of not knowing.

The medication I took still wasn't enough to control the symptoms of these two chronic pain diseases. The doctor instructed John on how to administer the EPI injections of *Enbrel®*.

This weekly injection/medication is supposed to help block the signals that cause joint pain and swelling in AS patients. It's a very painful injection given in either the arms, legs, or stomach. I'd put a rag in my mouth to prevent the kids from hearing my painful sounds when I received the shots. I may sound like a baby, but these diseases heightened my nerves and pain levels more than usual. Once the injection kicked in, the pain was tolerable most times for about two to three days out of seven. With that, it gave me a chance to do more than I had been able to do prior to the injections. Believe it or not, I looked forward to those horrible painful injections to give me just a little relief. Unfortunately, I still had memory problems, fatigue, and depression. The memory problems were becoming embarrassing for me, especially when I was in public. My doctor said many patients with AS also share difficulties with memory loss. For this reason, I wasn't comfortable going out much. I normally was a social person, but not anymore.

My pain progressed and I started to hurt whenever anyone would touch my body. Even when the children would gently lean up against me to watch TV it hurt. I would persevere through the pain to have quality time with the children and to touch them with love. At that time, they didn't know how much I suffered. We are a very loving, hugging family, and I love all of our children so much that I knew their needs were more important than mine. I knew it was up to me to *"suck-it-up"* without letting them know how much it truly hurt.

The children tried to help me as much as they could. They would lay with me at times and make me nice, *"Hope you feel better soon, Mom."*

cards, or make me homemade jewelry to put a smile on my face. They were so cute.

When I couldn't go to a game, awards ceremony, parade, or whatever was important to them, I would be home alone crying. I love our children, and it broke my heart not to be able to be there for... their everything. I felt so bad for John. I felt so much guilt watching him do everything alone. He didn't sign up for this when we married. He was and still is an amazing man. He kept up with the demands but not without exhaustion. His parents lived fairly close to us and helped when they could. John was dad, mom, and my caregiver for three and a half years. I knew too well what it took to run our family and work a full-time job. I was hurting inside more than outside; it was tearing me up. John was accomplishing a never-ending list of to-dos. He even made sure he had the children dressed and ready for church every Sunday. To me, he often looked tired, but he never complained. He was and still is my hero.

CHAPTER 10

TOUCHED BY THE LORD

I was tired. Not just tired of the diseases, but tired of the many troublesome symptoms attached to them. At the same time, it killed me inside thinking our family would never be as it was when we all did wonderful things together.

Many people felt helpless; they didn't know what to say to me when they were around me. I undoubtedly had little to contribute to conversations, since I spent most of my days in a hot tub John bought me to help relieve painful pressure. Or I'd be in bed, or on the couch due to the hellacious pain. I wasn't up on current affairs during that time, nor was I interested in taking on the world's problems. I wanted to try to focus on positive, humorous TV shows. I had enough struggles pulling me down, so a few laughs here and there were good medicine in my eyes.

Rarely did I get to watch a full movie before falling asleep. I was miserable missing out on life with family, friends, our children, grandchildren and quality time with my best friend, my husband. I loathed my new life.

THE BREAKING POINT

My diseases continued to torture me physically and emotionally for three and a half years. I felt like I was a prisoner in my own body. I saw my body and motions as those of a much older individual, especially when the pain was so bad I was forced to use a walker or someone had to push me in a wheelchair. I hated passing a mirror, because I no longer recognized the person looking back at me. I cried more times during my illness than I had in my entire life.

My body and life had become a big, beastly nightmare. When I took a shower, the pain in my neck was so excruciating I had to rest my head against the shower wall to wash my hair. I'd even have to rest my arms before completing my hair washing. It was essential to be creative to achieve things needing to get done. I wanted to do some things on my own, and this was just another way of surviving without feeling I was imposing on my husband and others to wash my hair. I was feeling helplessness, frustration, and guilt for not being able to keep up. It made me more determined to do some things on my own. I used to be an independent woman and I didn't want pity. Physically and emotionally, I was being challenged. Sometimes to try to get relief, I would alternate my heating pad from one hip to the other, because that strange lady in black was right. Regrettably, I was having problems with my hips, a dreadful unbelievable level 9 out of 10 on the pain scale in my hips.

I was thankful for the glorious day when John surprised me with that hot tub. Seeing it brought me to tears. Heat was supposed to provide some relief, and it did; it was delightful. I used it every day and sometimes more than once a day for that temporary pain relief.

As far as my friends were concerned, after my healing they told me they didn't recognize me when I was ill. They saw the dramatic change in my weight due to my medications and lack of activity. They also said they could see the pain written all over my face. And I thought I was hiding the pain from people when I smiled.

An elderly couple, probably in their late 80's, swiftly walked past me as I had just left one of my doctor's appointments. After seeing the doctor and having him poke, push, and manipulate my body, strolling down the hallway with my walker was a challenge. Wow, that sweet elderly couple passing me was a reality check on where I was with my illness.

I knew I was in trouble having these two major chronic diseases. I had no idea how bad it would get, and I often prayed nobody else in the family would ever suffer the things I'd endured. I was at the end of what I could handle; I was ready to call my Heavenly Father for help. The doctors had done all they could do for me, and it wasn't enough. I was becoming an unhappy, pain ravaged individual. I barely called my life living, while I missed out on so many beautiful moments with my wonderful family. I wasn't building the great, fun, fond memories like we did prior to these diseases attacking me. I could no longer bear this burden on my own.

Our family lives by the Lord's promise in **Romans 8:28.** *"**And we know that in all things God works for the good of those who love Him, who have been called according to His purpose.**"* I needed my Father's help now more than ever. I needed Him to take this pain, and everything attached to it. After reading so many books about people being healed, even people suffering with stage 4 cancer, and people suffering with mental agony, I knew I was ready to ask the Lord for a healing. I was ready to be pain free.

Although I didn't want to be pitied, I could see people's reactions when they saw me. I didn't want to impose my illness on the minds of others anymore. I didn't want the children to be without a full time mother anymore and my husband without his best friend, forever girlfriend, and wife. I know my husband felt bad for me, but it was out of his control. I dearly appreciate him and the love he exemplified through the duration of my disabilities. I decided these diseases attacking me were no longer going to claim control over my life.

PRAYING WITH MORE THAN WORDS

First thing I did was talk to John. I explained my quest to ask our Lord for a healing, but first I was going to wean myself off all my medications. He told me he wanted me to talk to all my doctors about my plan. I told John I intended to speak with them prior to starting the weaning process. He expressed some concerns he had about what to expect, once my body was free of these meds I had been taking for so long, especially how it was going to affect me physically and emotionally. I understood his concerns, which was why I wanted to be careful about giving myself adequate time to properly wean off all meds. Of course, it is highly dangerous to go off medications' cold turkey, and I would never recommend anybody do such a thing. I hadn't read anything about anybody doing this with their medications, but I felt it was what I needed to do to be cured. I wanted to prove to Christ that His healing for me would be done with a pure body released from foreign chemicals. I knew I would be bedridden until the healing, and I was prepared to suffer short-term for the long-term glorious results. I also knew this was how it had to be done for me. I'm not saying this is how it should be done for others wanting to be healed, and I'm certainly not suggesting others follow my protocol. But, I can say, talk to your doctors if you are going to take control and allow the Lord to heal you.

My ankylosing spondylitis disease was a severe case compared to others I've spoken to who are suffering with AS. I guess it affects people differently. I'm sure having acute fibromyalgia on top of the AS exacerbated the degree of pain I suffered. I kept hoping it would go back into remission to give me a break, but it had not at that point. When I spoke to my doctors, I'm sure they thought I was crazy, but I really didn't care. I knew the Lord would heal me. I knew I couldn't have medication in my system if I believed in His miracles. The doctors did say if I needed anything they would be available for me. I was thankful for their gestures, but I knew my journey wouldn't need any help, except through my Lord and Savior, Jesus Christ.

Several weeks of weaning myself off all my medications left me completely incapacitated and confined to my bed. I dreaded every minute of it, especially the times I got out of bed to go to the bathroom. My body was at a breaking point, my emotions were frail, and I realized it was ultimately time to talk to Jesus.

I GIVE THIS TO YOU LORD

LIFTING IT UP 100% THROUGH PURE FAITH

On my first night, I prayed to be forgiven of all my sins. I prayed, *"I am heartily sorry for ever offending You Lord. I surrender all of my fears and ego."* Then I concluded with, *"I give this to You Lord."* After my prayer I went to sleep and, in the morning, I woke up still in horrific pain. The same results happened after the second night of saying the same prayer. Then, on the third night, when John came to bed, I was crying. Very concerned, he asked, *"What's wrong sweetheart?"* I explained to John what I was saying to the Lord as I prayed for a healing. I conveyed the words I used, *"I surrender all my fears and ego to You Lord"*, and sadly expressed how I still wasn't healed. John quickly interrupted and replied, *"No you didn't!"* I was shocked at his response. Then he clarified empathetically, *"Sweetheart, you have been in so much pain for so long, you're still expecting to be in pain when you wake up. You are not releasing it to the Lord."* Wow, I'm a logical person and his words truly resonated with me.

That night I said exactly the same things I had said the two prior nights. The only difference was that I spoke from my heart and not just my mouth. When I said, *"I surrender all my fears and ego,"* I added with my heart as I released it to Him, *"and I give this to You, Lord."* When I surrendered myself and the diseases, I raised my arms up in the air towards the ceiling of my bedroom. I completely lifted the diseases to Our Heavenly Father. I felt peaceful knowing I no longer owned this, I knew now it was in Jesus' hands. After this prayer I calmly went to sleep. When I woke in the morning, I was expecting to be free of pain instead of seeing if I was still in pain. There is a huge difference between the two. I knew wholeheartedly the Lord had heard my prayer and released me from the agony I'd endured for so long from these debilitating diseases. I immediately knew upon waking up, the Lord healed me. There was no pain, no fear or stress over my illnesses. I didn't need a walker or a wheelchair. And when my feet hit the floor **pain free** for the first time in three and a half years, *I praised Jesus!* I could have easily done a dance. I smiled and spoke aloud as I clasped my hands together in a prayerful position, *"Thank* *you, Jesus, for healing me! Thank you, thank you, thank you Jesus."* I was happy and I knew the Lord was pleased I trusted Him to relieve me of all my adversities through my faith in Him.

I repeated this prayer a few times joyfully. I prayed for a long time just thanking our Lord for answering my prayer and rejoiced eagerly wanting to tell the world how great He is! All glory goes to God!

As promised and found in, *https://bible.usccb.org/bible/james/5*
> **James 5:15** *and the prayer of "faith" will save the sick person, and the Lord will raise him up. If he has committed any sins, he will be forgiven.*

Many times, throughout my illness, my husband and I would pray for answers regarding what was occurring inside my body creating so much pain. And that prayer was answered when the doctor tested me for AS. We often prayed for a healing for me, however I wasn't healed until I completely surrendered my illness in faith to Him. I simply let it go and gave it all to the Lord. This is why I titled the book, *"I Give this to You, Lord."*

OTHERS HEALED INSPIRED ME

To me, after reading and researching testimonies from countless stories of others healed by our Lord, I know without hesitation He can heal people even in stage 4 cancer, paralysis or crippling disorders. I've witnessed the miracle of a crippled young lady's body being healed and transformed before my eyes on an old video in a church. It was a video that wasn't tampered with, because people didn't have the capability to do that back then. Technology was scarce at the time when I saw it.

As the young girl was assisted out of her wheelchair, she swayed side to side and fumbled as she attempted to walk with guidance. The few people present in the video were praying together for her to be healed. As they continued in prayer, I could literally see the child's distorted crippled

I GIVE THIS TO YOU LORD

legs straightening out until the girl could walk correctly. I believe I was meant to see that video for the purpose of sharing this miracle with all the readers here. The video was so old and I'm not sure what country it was made in. I have tried finding it, but haven't been successful in my search. At any rate, how about it, Praise Jesus for her glorious miraculous healing, AMEN!

In one of the books I read on miraculous healing testimonies, one unique testimony stood out to me. A woman was diagnosed with stage 4 cervical cancer. Doctors told her she didn't have long to live. When she returned home alone, she wept and prayed for a healing. She claimed to have received an angelic message that told her, "Fill the bathtub with water and sit in it." She realized this was a message from an angel and did exactly as she was instructed to do. While sitting in the water she could see a blackness coming from her privates. She was amazed as she watched the cancer leaving her body. She knew the Lord had heard her prayers and healed her. And when she went for her next tests, they all came back perfectly fine. Doctors had to claim it as a miracle. No more cancer. Amen, amen, thank you sweet Jesus!

I believe if you have physical illnesses, mental illnesses, emotional issues, or addictions, God can heal you if you desire to be healed and ***trust Him through your faith***. I've read many testimonies about people having addictions or mental illnesses being healed, so I know it too is possible. Those who believe in Jesus as their Savior and Healer, can surrender their bodies to the Lord. Let go of the fears and ego, and place them in Jesus' hands! Remember to repent from your sins to the Lord before asking for your healing. He loves each one of us and is waiting for us to call on Him for help, purely through our faith and trust in Him. And most importantly, never forget to thank Him for your healing.

Bottom line, if you are ready to be healed, use your faith, strength, wisdom, and courage and believe He can heal you too! *You are worthy, you are His child.* Remember, do not just use your words like I did many times, lift it up to Him, release it to Him, speak from the depths of your soul. If you have just one doubt in your mind, then don't bother asking to be healed.

DARLENE M. LINK

If you don't think you deserve it, then don't ask, because you are wrong and until you realize that you cannot be healed. The Lord just needs your heart to be truly sorry for your sins and promise to follow in His footsteps by trying to be more like Him. Then share your testimony with others.

Here are just a few book references written by individuals as they share their testimonies of dying and then returning back to life.
- *90 Minutes in Heaven by Don Piper with Cecil Murphey,*
- *23 Minutes in Hell by Bill Wiese*
- *Near Death Experiences to Hell and Back by John Graden*
  You can also find an article online written by Matt McWilliams on December 30, 2020, who wrote: "10 People Who Have Been to Hell and Their Stories", https://answersforeveryone.com/10-people-who-have-been-to-hell/

There are countless testimonies all over the world of people terribly ill, nearing death's door, yet they were healed. A dear friend and soul sister of mine was hours from death due to cancer throughout her body. Her family surrounded her bed and began praying for a healing. And it was done. Since her healing she has done incredible things to help others. Thank God for her faith and the faith of her family. All glory goes to Jesus for hearing and answering their prayers!

Some people say they are faithful, and have strong faith in our Lord, but they don't realize there is another level of that meaning: an unconditional trust in what the Mighty Lord can do and has to offer us. If only we all believed and realized His love for all of us is genuinely pure.

God does not give us cancer or other diseases; the darker forces have free will to do this to us and sometimes we do it to ourselves or we are victims of our environment, i.e.: mold, chemicals, contaminated water, etc. We need to take care of ourselves, because we can't smoke for years and expect not to advance in health issues, like asthma, COPD, or lung cancer. The warning signs are there. Besides, we are supposed to treat our body as a temple of God. If we feel we have not kept our bodies well, we need to ask God for forgiveness for not taking good care of our temple. Again, use your heart, not just words when asking the Lord for something so wonderfully powerful as a healing. Treat your temple/body with respect, as God has asked of us many times in the Bible.

Bible verse example: Our body, a temple of God:
https://bible.usccb.org/bible/1corinthians/3

>**Corinthians 3:16-17** *Do you not know that you are the temple of God, and that Spirit of God dwells in you? If anyone destroys God's temple, God will destroy that person; for the temple of God, which you are, is holy.*

It's up to us to reach out for Jesus' help and guidance throughout our journey in life. If anyone has not taken care of their body, ask the Lord for forgiveness, and strength. He will know if the intentions are pure.

After my healing, I quickly discovered I was in a new world. Because He also left me with gifts I never had before my healing, that only could have come from the purity of being touched by the Lord. When you receive Jesus and trust in the Lord you will be in awe. I smiled all the time. I can't express how glorifying it is to know how much God loves His children and is eager to release them from their illnesses. I cannot guarantee or promise everyone asking for a healing will be healed, but I do know the angels message said this book will help people. All Glory be to God!

CHAPTER 11

A WORLD WITH NEW EYES

*W*hy hadn't I seen this before? It's amazingly beautiful! Colors are more brilliant, and my senses are more attuned to the wonderful world God created for us. Is life so busy? Was I so absorbed in my life and other things I considered more important than the wonders that surrounds all of us every day? How could I have possibly missed it? Our world is astonishingly exquisite!

> **Ecclesiastes 3:11,** *He has made everything beautiful in his time. He has also set eternity in the human heart; yet no one can fathom what god has done from beginning to end.*
> **https://homilysunday.com/bible-verses/15-on-beauty-to-admire-the-creation-of-god-and-everything-on-it/**

A WHOLE NEW WORLD

I was physically filled with more joy, love, and peace than ever before. I had a goofy smile on my face all the time; I couldn't get rid of it, and quite honestly, I didn't want to. My demeanor had always been full of love for people, and I'd often smile, but now those feelings have become magnified to a profound sense of love greater than I knew was possible.

I have a burning desire to help others to be healed like I was healed. I've developed a philosophical appreciation for the many blessings I have—and have had—in my life. After taking in this new spiritual love experience, I realized just how blessed I was to have my eyes and heart opened. And now it's my turn to share my testimony with the world so others can also experience these wonders.

After the Lord touched me, I would literally stop and smell the flowers. I'd check out the bugs and watch them doing what they were created to do for our ecosystem. I enjoyed watching the colors of the seasons change. I valued watching the fall leaves turning from greens to yellows, oranges, reds, and browns. And although I had always loved the ocean as my happy place, it is mind-blowing to think about the complexity of how the ocean miraculously functions. When I think of the ocean, or sit on the beach listening to the forceful crashing waves, I think of the dynamics of how powerful and mighty it is, just like our Lord's strength and power. Isn't He so wonderful? Thank you, God, for creating such an astonishing, peaceful place for our temporary home. Praise God! If only God's children could be more like Him, then they would respectfully appreciate all these gifts He created for us.

When I share my testimony, I love challenging people to leave behind their electronics, go outside, breathe slowly, and relax to turn down their busy lives a bit. I hope they will see what I see, and appreciate what I've experienced. Go ahead and smell the flowers, watch the birds, listen to their lovely songs, and observe the picturesque beauty before them. Go ahead and touch nature with your hands and heart.

I started taking an interest in photographing nature. I wanted to keep it with me forever and share it with others. I became a camera junky, in love with everything. The sunrises and sunsets were things I looked forward to watching. And where John and I live now gives us a beautiful view of God's outstanding sunsets. I have countless pictures of the many colors with which each sunset dazzles the skies.

Another thing that is prevalent from being healed is to focus more on the positive things' life has to offer. I surround myself with positive people and release myself from people who are toxic and want to cause drama. It's critical for us to surround ourselves with positive people to become better people ourselves, regardless of how hard it is to break from those we love who are not so positive. However, we should not hide from people, because we need to do God's work in spreading His messages in hopes to bring them closer to the Lord.

ANGELIC MESSAGE

Having received an angelic message, I could clearly hear— *"Write a book. It will help people."* I wondered what the Lord wanted me to include in this book. *What am I going to write about? Where do I start?*

The very next day, when I was involved in a project, not even thinking about the book, I went to the second floor of our home to get a ruler near the loft overlooking the family room. While there, I clearly heard the words coming from the TV in the family room below, *"If you are writing a book, just write what you know."* I stopped what I was doing and rushed to the railing, nearly falling over, to look below at the TV. Nobody was in the family room at that moment, but the TV was on, and I heard this message *LOUD* and *CLEAR*, as if the volume had been amplified to get my attention. Then, as I was watching in amazement, the same lady on the "Book TV" station was telling a group of people how to write a book and repeated her message, *"If you are writing a book, just write what you know."* She concluded, *"It's as simple as that."* I couldn't even understand why this station was on; we never watched shows on Book TV. Still shocked, I knew without a doubt the message was intended for me, because this angel really knew how to deliver a message at the right time. *So, I was "at the right place at the right time" (God's place, God's time).*

CHAPTER 12

GOD'S PLAN FOR US

If you've ever wondered, *does God have a plan for me?* I'm here to tell you, *He does!* You might spend years wondering what it is and why He hasn't provided it yet, but then, at a particular moment in your life, He will reveal your plan to you. It's up to all of us to listen and trust in His plan for us. In some cases, I believe people have listened and are already living their life's purpose, which is God's will.

LISTENING FOR OPPORTUNITIES

Some people magnanimously choose careers out of compassion, like wanting to become a doctor/nurse to help people, or courageously choosing to be a firefighter/police officer/paramedic. Perhaps someone feels they have been chosen to take a selfless position as a religious leader, and dedicate their life to serving the Lord through His teachings. In cases like those, it may appear they are doing exactly what God intended. Unfortunately, we must keep in mind that not everyone in these positions is fulfilling them for the love of the Lord; sometimes they have ulterior motives not in God's plan. A few of those reasons could be power, greed, or cleverly luring in the innocent for their own self-centered desires that are certainly not under God's design.

I believe, in most cases, these individuals are where they need to be, or where God intended them to land with their career choice, so He can use them in multiple ways. God may have chosen them so He could lead others in their direction for guidance through their resources and expertise. When others are led to these people, He may be offering them something of great importance that can alter their lives in a favorable way, much like, *"Being at the right place, at the right time"*, or more likely, *"God's place, God's time."* I've experienced and witnessed it often. Perhaps many of you have, as well. God leads specific people into our paths to answer our prayers or prayers of loved ones. God knows us well and if we listen, we can give more to our brothers and sisters through divine intervention. Sometimes it's good when we stop and notice the people surrounding us by giving them a simple gesture of praise. It could lead to greater strides and self-assurance for another. In fact, I believe some people reading this book or who have purchased it for someone they felt needed a healing was not by chance, I believe God led them to the book to experience their own miracle. But, it has to be through complete trust in our Lord to remove it from them. They have to let it go, surrender it to Him.

Q: What happens to others when we do or don't pay attention to them?

A: Sometimes absolutely nothing. And other times it can be critical and life changing for them. Below are two examples of how the Lord directed these individuals to John and I to get them the help or answers troubling them. Giving time and listening to someone can make a world of difference..

Example 1: *My husband taught advanced math at a high school. One day a student asked to speak to him after class. He always made himself available for students when they needed to talk or help with math. She shared her abusive home situation and asked for help. My husband helped her to report the abuse, and through the proper channels was able to get the assistance needed to improve her home life situation.*

Example 2: *A young lady had questions about God and asked me if I had time to talk to her. I did have a list of things to do that day, but pushed them aside without her knowing. She asked a lot of* *questions, and we spoke for a long time. The conversation was productive, and she started going to church to learn more about her Creator.*

We don't know what the outcome of these two situations would have been had we not taken the time to listen to these young ladies. What's important is the Lord knew, and we were thankful He led them in our direction.

ACCEPTING THE PATH

Sometimes God's paths are so powerful they can forever alter people's lives in a positive way.

Bible example:
https://www.biblegateway.com/passage/?search=John%204-42&version=NIV

> **John: 4:42** *4 Now he (Jesus) had to go through Samaria. 5 So he came to a town in Samaria called Sychar, near the plot of ground Jacob had given to his son Joseph. 6 Jacob's well was there, and Jesus, tired as he was from the journey, sat down by the well. It was about noon. 7 When a Samaritan woman came to draw water, Jesus said to her, "Will you give me a drink?" 8 (His disciples had gone into the town to buy food.) 9 The Samaritan woman said to him, "You are a Jew and I am a Samaritan woman. How can you ask me for a drink?" (For Jews do not associate with Samaritans.) 10 Jesus answered her, "If you knew the gift of God and who it is that asks you for a drink, you would have asked him and he would have given you living water." 11 "Sir," the woman said, "you have nothing to draw with and the well is deep. Where can you get this living water? 12 Are you greater than our father Jacob, who gave us the well and drank from it himself, as did also his sons and his livestock?" 13 Jesus*

answered, "Everyone who drinks this water will be thirsty again, 14 but whoever drinks the water I give them will never thirst. Indeed, the water I give them will become in them a spring of water welling up to eternal life." 15 The woman said to him, "Sir, give me this water so that I won't get thirsty and have to keep coming here to draw water." 16 He told her, "Go, call your husband and come back." 17 "I have no husband," she replied. Jesus said to her, "You are right when you say you have no husband. 18 The fact is, you have had five husbands, and the man you now have is not your husband. What you have just said is quite true." 19 "Sir," the woman said, "I can see that you are a prophet. 20 Our ancestors worshiped on this mountain, but you Jews claim that the place where we must worship is in Jerusalem." 21 "Woman," Jesus replied, "believe me, a time is coming when you will worship the Father neither on this mountain nor in Jerusalem. 22 You Samaritans worship what you do not know; we worship what we do know, for salvation is from the Jews. 23 Yet a time is coming and has now come when the true worshipers will worship the Father in the Spirit and in truth, for they are the kind of worshipers the Father seeks. 24 God is spirit, and his worshipers must worship in the Spirit and in truth." 25 The woman said, "I know that Messiah" (called Christ) "is coming. When he comes, he will explain everything to us." 26 Then Jesus declared, "I, the one speaking to you—I am he." The Disciples Rejoin Jesus 27 Just then his disciples returned and were surprised to find him talking with a woman. But no one asked, "What do you want?" or "Why are you talking with her?" 28 Then, leaving her water jar, the woman went back to the town and said to the people, 29 "Come, see a man who told me everything I ever did. Could this be the Messiah?" 30 They came out of the town and made their way toward him. 31 Meanwhile his disciples urged him, "Rabbi, eat something." 32 But he said to them, "I have food to eat that you know nothing about." 33 Then his disciples said to each other, "Could someone have brought him food?" 34 "My food," said Jesus, "is to do the will of him who sent me and to finish his work. 35 Don't you have a saying, 'It's still four months until harvest'? I tell you, open your eyes and look at the fields! They are ripe for harvest. 36 Even now the one who reaps draws a wage and harvests a crop for eternal life, so that the sower and the reaper may be glad together. 37 Thus the saying 'One sows and another reaps' is true. 38 I sent you to reap what you have not worked for. Others have done the hard work, and you have reaped the benefits of their labor." Many Samaritans Believe 39 Many of the Samaritans from that town believed in him because of the woman's testimony, "He told me everything I ever did." 40 So when the Samaritans came to him, they urged him to stay with them, and he stayed two days. 41 And because of his words many more became believers. 42 They said to the woman, "We no longer believe just because of what you said; now we have heard for ourselves, and we know that this man really is the Savior of the world."

Jesus could have taken other paths, but he deliberately chose to go through Samaria to encounter the woman whom He knew she was considered unclean, where He demonstrates his intention to reach those considered outcasts and marginalized, even when it meant crossing social boundaries to do so.

God knows what He's doing. He knows what is in our hearts, good or bad. He also knows what's in our thoughts, even though we may never speak of them to others.

We don't need a big title, college degree, or even a decent education to follow God's plan. Our lifestyle, ethnicity or creed does not make us different or less worthy. To God, we are all His children, and He loves each of us deeply and equally. So, whoever we are, when we're helping others with the things that deeply touch our souls, we are glorifying God.

That is our mission while we are on Earth, our temporary home. We should periodically ask ourselves this question: *"At this moment, if I took my last breath, am I comfortable with my life's choices?"* I've heard people jokingly say, *"I plan on living a long life!"* Or more seriously, *"My family has longevity so, with most of my relatives living well into their 90's, I'm sure I'll be around for a long time."* However, life is not an exact science. This is, again, God's plan, and when He is ready to bring us home, we will go. Ready or not, it's happening with no chance of saying, *"Oh wait, I need a little more time."* Death isn't something we can foresee; at any moment we could take our last breath. We should categorically never be so sure that tomorrow will come.

Once when I went to the hospital I broke out in a sweat then passed out in the emergency room. My blood pressure was 50/30, I had a fever, and excruciating pain in my lower right side. A kidney stone was discovered and surgery removed the stone. I also was told I had sepsis. I was in the hospital for a week to regain strength and good health. My husband was told that one more hour and I probably wouldn't be here. So, with the several close encounters with death I've had, I never take my days for granite.

MAKING CRITICAL CHOICES IN LIFE

Popularity is fun, exciting, and provocative for many people as a goal in life. The entertainment world is a perfect example. It may or may not be in our favor when we stand before the Lord for final judgement. It's a critical time for all of us to make good, respectful decisions for ourselves and not for the show or popularity of others. Just because, *"we can"* or *"everyone is doing it,"* doesn't mean, *"we should."* Daily we should work on our shortcomings and build on things we are compassionate about, such as mentoring the youth *(who knows how powerful a simple conversation with a teenager needing help could be, it could save their life)*, caring for an elderly person that feels like a burden to others *(we can make them feel needed and important when they have no control over their situation)* and helping to feed the hungry. As humanitarians, we should do our best to help the less fortunate or troubled souls seeking guidance towards a better tomorrow.

Scripture reminds us what we should be doing to help those who are hungry and less fortunate: ***https://biblehub.com***

Proverbs 14:31 *"Whoever oppresses a poor man insults his Maker, but he who is generous to the needy honors Him."*

Proverbs 22:9 *"Whoever has a bountiful eye will be blessed, for He shares His bread with the poor."*

Proverbs 28:27 *"Whoever gives to the poor will not want, but he who hides his eyes will get many a curse."*

Proverbs 31:20 *"She opens her hand to the poor and reaches out her hands to the needy."*

Isaiah 61:1 *"The Spirit of the Lord GOD is upon me, because the LORD has anointed me to bring good news to the poor; He has sent me to bind up the brokenhearted, to proclaim liberty to the captives, and the opening of the prison to those who are bound…"*

Matthew 19:21 *"Jesus said to him, "If you would be perfect, go, sell what you possess and give to the poor, and you will have treasure in heaven; and come, follow me."*

These are just a few examples of His teachings. Let us help the oppressed to follow His teachings? We know of people that have given food and drinks to anyone begging for food on the street. As well as delivering blankets for the homeless, donated coats, gloves, scarves and hats. Those receiving these blessings are so grateful for the help.

Other ways to show our love are; rescuing children by reporting serious suspicion of child abuse instead of sitting silently while someone could be destroying their inner being for life. We can also help guide individuals to safety from battered homes. These are just a few examples of proactive love. There is so much we can do, like; help rape victims from further abuse, help animals from abuse, teach someone to read and write, tutor ill homebound students, giving up one of our possessions to someone who really needs it, donate blood to save lives, help our soldiers who sacrifice their lives to protect our land and freedom rights, and help our own church to give the pastor/priest/minister a break or invite them to dinner to get to know them better and see where you can help them, and the list of options goes on and on. Listen to your heart to discover where you can give. Whatever you feel passionate about is probably your purpose.

As for myself, I wasn't certain what my purpose in life was, even though I've always tried to be helpful to others in need. I do adore children and thought helping them was my purpose. God may have more than one purpose for us; we could have multiple purposes for serving the Lord. Again, we just need to be open to the signs and follow our hearts.

I know He wants all of us to follow His Commandments so we can be the best we can to honor Him. Whom should we strive harder to give praise and honor than God?

While we are here in this temporary home, we should learn from our mistakes, become disciplined individuals before facing judgment day. It's a lifelong lesson for all of us, regardless of what status we attain in this life. Even the most religious people in this world have faults; we are human, and nobody is perfect. It's important to remember in **Romans: 3:23** Paul wrote, **"For all have sinned and fall short of the glory of God."** Yes, we all make mistakes, we learn, we ask for forgiveness, we correct or reduce our faults, and improve ourselves to become better, Godlier people. To me this is the meaning of what a human soul's cycle of life should be, and what God is looking for in all of us. We will be face to face with Our Creator today, tomorrow, or years from now. We can't get away from that inevitable final day of judgment. It's never too late to make positive changes in our hearts or repent from our past behavior.

I believe He is using me and many others to spread our testimonies of His Word for people willing to listen.

MY PURPOSE

After my angelic message, it was important for me to share my testimony with all who read this book. My healing is one of the most important things to share at this point in my life. He wanted others to know they too can be healed. Even you can be healed according to God's words in the Bible.

I'm not going to say others healed will experience the same things I have experienced, because each of us are unique in our own way. God knows our capabilities, even if we don't know what they are yet. When a person is healed, they too *may* see the world as beautiful as it was intended for all of us.

At times, the Lord uses people to write their experiences and stories to help others understand His messages and love for all. One thing is certain, He wants me to express to everyone that He is here for us. Nobody is treated differently or more special based on his or her livelihood, financial status, lifetime certificates, awards, goals, fame, or anything else they may have accomplished. What matters is that we ask for forgiveness for our past sins and work towards a healthier new path for ourselves from this moment forward. Pray for forgiveness for any current flaws or flaws from the past. Ask God to remove any hate inside your heart and fill that void with His love. Ask the Lord to give you the strength and wisdom to do His Will without repeating flaws after asking for forgiveness for them. If we ask for forgiveness, and then purposely repeat any offensive acts, that is not pleasing to our Lord, and it shows we are not sorry for our sin(s). We all should work on our flaws until they are no longer a part of our lives. There is nothing wrong with asking for help if we struggle with the challenges of repeating our sins. Then, let in His love and trust He will be there for us. The power of faith goes a long way, it's not just a word, it's a way of living and believing that makes miracles happen.

DARLENE M. LINK

Scriptures in Matthew 14:22-33 teaches us how important our faith in Him is when we believe. https://usccb.org/bible/matthew/14

Matthew 14:22-33, *Then he made the disciples get into the boat and precede him to the other side, while he dismissed the crowds, 23 after doing so he went up on the mountain by himself to pray. When it was evening he was there alone. 24 Meanwhile the boat, already a few miles offshore, was being tossed about by the waves, for the wind was against it. 25 During the fourth watch of the night, he came toward them, walking on the sea. 26 When the disciples saw him walking on the sea they were terrified. "Is it a ghost," they said, and they cried out in fear. 27 At once (Jesus) spoke to them, "Take courage, it is I; do not be afraid." 28 Peter said to him in reply, "Lord, if it is you, command me to come to you on the water." 29 He said, "Come." Peter got out of the boat and began to walk on the water towards Jesus. 30 But when he saw how {strong} the wind was he became frightened; and, beginning to sink, he cried out, "Lord, save me!" 31 Immediately Jesus stretched out his hand and caught him, and said to him, "O you of little faith, why did you doubt?" 32 After they got into the boat, the wind died down. 33 Those, who were in the boat, did him homage, saying, "Truly, you are the Son of God."*

What can we learn from the account of Peter walking on water?

One of Jesus Christ's most instructive miracles takes place was when the apostle Peter jumps out of a boat and walks on turbulent water to meet the Lord on the sea. Not only does Jesus walk on the Sea of Galilee here, but Peter walks on the water as well. The disciples are beginning to see who Jesus is, but their faith in Him still has room for growth.
https://gotquestions.org/Peter-walking-on-water.html

We can also learn that Peter considered himself to be faithful to Jesus, but when he took his focus off of Jesus he doubted Him and began to sink into the sea. Many of us are very much like Peter. We feel we are strong in our faith, but lose focus and start doubting Him as well. I was guilty of this myself when I wasn't healed the first two nights after asking for a healing. I had to remove all of my fears and ego to allow Jesus to take over when I gave it to Him. What a powerful message Jesus taught us through this incredible scripture.

After my healing, the Lord gave me something I wasn't expecting. He only gives us what He knows we can handle. And I will follow Him wherever He asks me to go. I give all glory to our Lord. I've been given a unique mission. He had big plans for me, and I'm following it to serve Him. It took an open mind to do what he asked of me. He will not ask anything from us if He knows we cannot handle it, but if we believe He has, we need to ask for the strength to persevere through it, and it will be done by way of faith.

CHAPTER 13
ACCEPTING OUR GIFTS FROM JESUS

After Jesus healed me, I started knowing things before they happened, and I'd see places I'd never seen been, yet I could give details of the places before entering them. I knew other things too, like when one of my family members was going to have a tire blow out. Even though I told everyone to check their tires, our son did not. So, on his way home from the beach with friends, his tire had a blowout. Thank God they were fine. I was quite surprised as to how accurate these things were. I knew it was at the hands of our Lord who touched me.

Some of the things were quite pleasurable too. For example, the evening of my mother's Christmas party, our daughter Crystal and I stayed behind to help clean up. I was washing the dishes and Crystal was drying them. It was like a switch went on when I stood close to her. I instantly knew she was pregnant. With a silly big smile, I asked her, *"How are you doing?"* Surprised I asked her this question, she replied as she smiled back, "I'm fine!" I said, *"Good!"* Then she jokingly said, *"How are you?"* Laughing, I said, *"I'm doing great!"*

I wasn't sure if Crystal knew about her pregnancy, and I didn't want to spoil the surprise if she didn't, but as soon as she left to go home, I shared this exciting news with my mother and my husband, John. Within a couple days after the party, Crystal found out she was expecting. Immediately, she shared this glorious news with everyone. A few months later I placed my head near her small baby bump, then immediately lifted my head and sat straight up, exclaiming excitedly, *"Oh my, I know the gender of the baby."* I knew she didn't want to know, and quickly she said, *"Don't tell me, I want to be surprised."* I knew it was her last child she was planning on having and I completely understood, but I still had to confide in my husband and mother privately that she was having a girl. I was so excited for her! When she delivered Rosanna (Rosie), she was beautiful. In addition to these feelings, I had many other experiences too.

Without a doubt, these were things I never experienced prior to my healing—definitely a Godly gift. Shortly afterward, I discovered my new paths and the destiny the Lord was preparing me for, and I knew I had to accept His direction. In addition, this unique change inside me confirmed my healing not just for my family and friends, but also for the non-believers that knew me and knew this was never a part of my pre-healed life.

I know all this sounds crazy, but I promise, I'm not a crazy person. If you are uncomfortable with these types of situations or don't believe in them because of your religious beliefs, please go to the next chapter. I promise the next chapter is one that will leave you with a positive feeling.

After my healing, I went to one of my doctors to share my healing testimony, and to my surprise, his response was, *"I know the mind is powerful and capable of doing great things."* Disappointed at the time, I didn't want to argue with someone who didn't believe in the miracles our Lord could bestow upon us, but now I would definitely challenge someone to help them see the Light.

USING THE GIFTS/BLESSINGS

Having these abilities gives no credit to me; they are all through the grace of our Lord. These different things happening to me were all so surreal in the beginning, especially, when I discovered I could do something called psychometry, which occurs when a person can hold an object or touch something that gives them images and knowledge of the history of that object. I first discovered it after I was at my aunt's house with my cousin. When his mother, my godmother, passed away, family members could come to her house to pick out something of hers to treasure. I looked around and picked up a rectangular black sheer scarf with beautiful, delicate, white, embroidered flowers embellishing the edges. I immediately saw my aunt wearing it in church at a funeral and instantly knew this was what she wore at funerals. It was shocking and emotional. I told my cousin this was what I wanted, but I didn't share my experience with him. It was my first time experiencing anything like that and I was trying to comprehend what had just happened to me. I wore the scarf at her funeral in honor of her. I've worn it at most funerals since.

My second psychometry encounter was when our daughter Stephanie was packing to move to Georgia to be with her boyfriend, Jason. While I was helping her pack, I picked up a photograph of Kyle, *(her boyfriend who had passed away in her arms a few years prior)*. As soon as I picked it up, I started tearing up and sobbing. I said, *"Oh my gosh, Kyle just told me to tell you he loves you and he's watching over you."* His energy was so strong and emotional. This was more than getting a connection to history; it was receiving her deceased boyfriend's message. I believe he could never relay this message if it weren't for the Lord allowing it to happen.

MESSAGE FROM HEAVEN

Kyle was a year older than Stephanie. They went to the same high school where they met. Kyle was in his senior year and Stephanie was a junior. The summer following his graduating year, one of Stephanie's friends' fathers took his daughter and two of her best friends on a weekend vacation with him to an oceanfront hotel. Stephanie was one of her best friends. The three girls and the father were in one city, whereas their boyfriends stayed at a hotel one city away from where they were staying. This way they could enjoy their time at the beach together.

On the first day the six friends and the father all went out to dinner. When they returned to the hotel, they all put on their swimsuits and hung out on the dock of the ocean front hotel. I called the father and asked how things were going and he said the kids had been sitting on the dock talking for hours and were having a great time. I told him I was glad to hear they were enjoying themselves and thanked him for inviting Stephanie.

Several hours later I received a devastating phone call from Stephanie screaming and crying, *"Kyle's dead, Kyle's dead."* I couldn't understand what she was saying but my husband was next to me and could clearly hear what she was saying. He told me and we were shocked to hear this dreadful news from our distraught daughter. She gave us the brief end of the story of what happened. It was such a horrible freaky accident. We told her we were on our way.

WHAT HAPPENED

While the kids were sitting on the dock for hours, Kyle spontaneously stood up and said he was hot and dove into the water to cool off. Unfortunately, none of them realized the tide had gone out while they spent hours talking and enjoying each other's time together. The water was shallow. Kyle instantly broke his neck and floated up. Stephanie said at first when Kyle floated on the water, they all thought he was playing around. Kyle liked a good joke. But this was no joke and they realized something was very wrong. Stephanie and all her friends jumped into the water immediately. Instantaneously they knew what had happened as they stood in the shallow ocean waters. Stephanie held him as he was dying in her arms. Everyone began screaming for help. It was a horrific dreadful experience that will forever haunt them when they think of that day. As an adult this would be so traumatizing, but a seventeen-year-old girl in love, it is beyond words to express such a life changing experience.

I GIVE THIS TO YOU LORD

When Stephanie was able to share that day with John and I, we listened compassionately. She started with their drive down to the beach in his car. A song about death came on the radio and Stephanie told Kyle she was afraid of dying. Kyle was a firefighter and his response to her was, *"If I died today, I would be fine with it. I'm not afraid of dying."* That day was so surreal to her, and when she thinks back on that day, she can't believe he spoke those words on the day he died. She also shared; it was the first time he told her he loved her. This was heartbreaking to hear, and we all sobbed while our hearts were broken for her and all those who loved him dearly. We were glad she was ready to talk about it because that is a part of the healing process of grieving. We did seek counseling for her to help cope. I believe this helped to some point.

Earlier on that dreadful day, yet glorious for Kyle, Stephanie took a picture of Kyle dressed in a nice shirt and khaki pants when they all went out to eat that evening. He was the only one in the picture and it was a full body great picture and memory for her and for his mother. Stephanie blew up the photo to an 8" x 10" picture and gave it to Kyle's mother. Stephanie also wrote a poem about Kyle, titled, *"My Hero"*. She also gave Kyles's mother a copy of her poem. When we arrived at the funeral home, his mother had the framed picture of Kyle, and the poem Stephanie wrote situated on Kyle's memorial table. I'm sure his mother will forever treasure the thoughtful gifts from Stephanie.

John and I had never seen so many people attend a funeral in our whole life as we did at Kyle's funeral. It looked like the whole fire department came, and a mountain of people from the school he just graduated from, including the principal and many teachers. Plus, his other friends outside his school and his extended family. He was a genuinely great guy, and this turnout certainly reflected his impact on the lives of others he left behind.

Kyles's mother asked us if Stephanie could spend the night at her place along with other family member guests. Of course, we had no objections if it was fine with Stephanie. Stephanie was touched by her invitation and accepted it.

Kyle's mother loved Stephanie. She told Stephanie to go into Kyle's room to pick out anything she wanted. Stephanie went into his bedroom and decided on 2 shirts. One was her favorite shirt on him, and the other still had his scent on it. Stephanie tacked his nice shirt to her bedroom wall. Then she added photos of her fondest memories of them together, as well as group shots of their friends. She slept with the other shirt with his scent on it for a couple of years. We felt this was healthy for her and a way of coping with such a loss.

A few weeks after his passing Stephanie and her friends decided to go camping. This was a weekend trip planned before Kyle passed. At first, they were going to cancel the trip, but then decided it would be something Kyle would want them to do. While camping around the fire, they talked a lot about Kyle. Through the stories they reminisced, Stephanie said, *"I think it was good for all of us, because we would cry and laugh and cry again about our times with Kyle."*

Overall, John and I thought this trip was the perfect remedy for all of them to share in their healing process together.

Years later Stephanie and Jason dressed up to match an affair at an annual Pirates Fest on the beach. While walking along the beach a bottle came ashore. Jason picked up the mysterious bottle and noticed a paper inside. Curiously, he opened the message which read, ***"I love you Isabella"***. This message brought chills to them, because Stephanie's costume included a wooden sword with the name *"Isabella"* engraved on it. We all believe it was a heavenly message gifted for Stephanie from Kyle. We realized he was still watching over her.

I GIVE THIS TO YOU LORD

**Stephanie & Jason
Isabella Sword**

I shared this story because it shows how things can fall in line with God's plans. Also, as I mentioned, this is a perfect example of how we never know when we will be leaving this world. We don't want to assume we have a long time before we pass, it's all up to our Lord when He wants us to come home.

What were the odds Kyle would say he wasn't afraid of dying, then die that day? And what are the odds he would tell Stephanie he loved her on that same day for the first time? God Almighty knew He was taking Kyle on that special day, and He knew Stephanie needed to hear those messages from Kyle before he was taken into the Lord's Kingdom. And the miracle of bringing a bottle to her feet on the ocean with the loving message. All coincidences or God's permission for Kyle to send?

DARLENE M. LINK

ASSISTING THE POLICE

Once, when a brutal murder and kidnapping took place in a nearby town, the spirit of the murdered woman communicated with me. She wanted my help.

So, in the situation of the departed spirit wishing to communicate with me, I felt I needed to see what I could do to help her. I contacted the detectives working on the case. Prior to my diseases I was a legal assistant at a law firm in town and was comfortable being around police and detectives. It was a little awkward asking them if I could help them in this case. I shared my healing story with them and how it's affected me. I let them know the woman was reaching out to me and I asked if I could go to the victim's crime scene. I also asked them if they could provide me with a couple of items to read, preferably a piece of jewelry and a piece of her clothing. The detectives were desperate for any leads on the case and permitted this request. So, they spoke with the sister of the victim to allow me into the home.

While at the victim's home, the sister was quite nervous and still distraught over the horrific murder of her sister. I hated putting her through this, I wished the detectives could have sent an officer to let me in, but I guess this was better than not getting in at all. And I'm sure they were working around the clock to capture this murderer.

When I went upstairs to the exact location where the attack took place, I chose to sit on the spot where the carpet was removed for DNA blood testing. As I sat there with the two items *(a necklace and a blouse)*, I closed my eyes and focused briefly before I started receiving messages she was giving me. It was like watching a movie; with my eyes closed I could see exactly what happened. I also physically felt the force behind the murder weapon on the back of my head for a brief moment and I saw what he did to her afterwards. It was horrible and incredibly sad. Unfortunately, I could also see the children witnessing the murder and how upset they were. It broke my heart they had to witness something so dreadfully traumatizing. The daughter was the one I was most concerned about because of her age. After speaking with a psychologist regarding my concerns for this child, she stated she would most likely need counseling to get through her traumatic experience. However, the baby boy was very young and hopefully will not remember the incident, despite his loud crying from the stressful screaming emotions going on at that moment.

After leaving I immediately typed up a full detailed report of my findings while it was fresh in my mind. After the detectives read my report, they asked if I had spoken with anyone regarding the case. I told them I spoke with nobody. They said my details were spot on and there was information I provided that was not public knowledge and only the two of them knew. I never read anything about the case prior to my report. Helping them would have never been possible if it weren't for our Lord allowing the victim to communicate to me for resolution in her case. So, praise God and all glory goes to Him for leading the victim to me to intercede in helping her. Her murderer is behind bars for the rest of his life.

I must admit a year prior to this first case I saw the legs of a young child behind a dumpster. I was scared at the time, because of having seven children of my own and it was an emotional sight. I pushed those images and thoughts out of my head. I couldn't handle that at the time. I told the Lord, if this was something He wanted me to do, to please give me the strength and emotional ability to handle it. When I was given this woman's connection, I was able to handle her case and all other connections from then on. I'm thankful Jesus answered my prayer and plea for help to accept the emotions associated with this path.

And, when I mentioned to the detectives about the little girl I saw behind the dumpster, they told me precisely what case it was and where it took place.

THE DREAM

A little girl came to the side of my bed where I was sleeping. I woke up to see her looking at me with her hand reaching out for me to take. I'd say she was between the ages of nine to eleven years old wearing period clothing that looked, to me, as if they she was from the early 1900's. I didn't feel threatened by her presence and took her hand as I got out of bed. Still holding hands, she guided me around my bed to exit my bedroom. Before leaving I looked back at my sleeping husband and thought about letting him know I would be back. But he looked so peaceful I chose not to disturb him. When we exited my bedroom, she guided us into a room to the right. Now if you leave my bedroom and go to the right, we'd end up in my bathroom. However, I was surprised to be in a bedroom with a pinkish misty heugh that appeared to be a child's bedroom, most likely her bedroom. Straight ahead was a child sized bed up against the wall where there was a window. The home was obvious to me as an old Victorian home. The little girl led me to the window, where I let go of her hand to lean over the bed to look outside. With the distance from the window to the ground I could tell this home was at least three stories high. With concerned emotions, I could see these three men in blue soldier uniforms abruptly walking towards the front of the house. Each man was gripping a musket gun with two hands. Immediately my motherly instinct kicked in and I was worried about this little girl. I knew these men were approaching with no good intention. The little girl was no longer in the room, so I ran out of the bedroom and swiftly headed down a winding stairway I found to the right of me when exiting the bedroom. As I reached halfway down the stairs I heard three loud gunshots. Stopping my motion, I instantly knew she and her family were killed. I woke up and to this day can vividly recall every detail as if it just happened.

This little girl was a spirit from a situation I was working on at the time. She and her family used to live at what is now a well-known establishment in Exton, Pennsylvania. After her visit, myself, a priest, and deacon went to the home/business establishment and the house was blessed. She and her family I believe are now at peace in their eternal home with Jesus.

I mention this story, because I believe God wanted them to be at peace and that's why He allowed her to communicate this message to me in a dream. In the Bible, Jesus recognized as *"ghosts"* and *"spirits"*.

> **Luke, 24:39** *Jesus said, "Look at My hands and My feet, it is I Myself; touch Me and see; a ghost does not have flesh and bones as you see I have."*
> *https://biblehub.com/niv/luke/24.htm*

Years ago, I questioned everything about what people would call *"haunted"*. About a year or so before my healing, my mother had just moved into a new home on a few acres in the country. My mom began telling me she had ghosts in her home. I kept telling her she was used to living in the suburbs and now that she was in the country, she was able to hear every little noise. She expressed defensively, there's more than just noises going on. It appeared I had an explanation for everything she shared with me. Well, that was until I had my very first ghostly/spirit experience, again, prior to my healing. While I was in her bathroom completely by myself, I was just about to flush the toilet when I felt fingers literally run through my hair, starting at the base of my neckline, and moving up my head. It was so real it felt like a live person literally was in the bathroom doing it. As I explained earlier, I'm not one to get scared. What happened to me was not threatening. I didn't feel pain. I wasn't pushed or scratched; it was just fingers gently going through my hair. I'm a logical person and fear wasn't needed.

When I came out of the bathroom, I sat calmly next to my mother, (Sandy) and apologized to her. I said, *"I believe you."* I shared my experience and told her I was now on the other side of the fence. I believed her 100% and was truly sorry for doubting her.

As time went by, things progressed in their home, and in their huge high ceiling two car garage, a four foot utility light began swinging back and forth on its own. Not like being moved by an air force, such as wind or an air conditioner, it moved like a child's swing. Some things were getting more bazaar. Objects would disappear, voices could be heard by my mom and Barry, as well as visitors/guests.

When my mother saw a dark figure in her bedroom, she screamed out and her husband Barry woke up to her scared shaking body. That's when they knew it was time to reach out to a paranormal team to investigate the home and property to see what was there.

Their home was investigated five times by five different paranormal teams. Because of the increase in activity and some very concerning things happening, they were desperate. Not one of the paranormal teams was able to give resolution to the situation. Each team validated the home and property to be haunted by multiple spirits and each team came up with the same names independently. They also said there was a demonic entity present. We pretty much knew that because of some of the incidents occurring in the home and on the property. One most unpleasant incident was when my mother was struck on her head by a black orb she said she saw come at her quickly. It did leave a mark on her head. Now, my mother at the time was in her mid-70's and didn't need this stress in her life. Even though none of the paranormal teams knew how to get rid of the demon or how to help the spirits, one team did do a smudging. Later I learned smudging was only a temporary fix. It only gets rid of the dark entity for a brief time. They do come back and are not happy when they return. If you ever watch paranormal teams on TV, pay attention to the cases who smudge a home. What you'll find is activity starts back up again after a few weeks to a few months and things are worse than before.

Because a demonic entity was in their home and on the property, I was fearful for my mother and Barry. They were not comfortable in their own home, and I feared for their safety.

When our Heavenly Father calls on us to do something we must answer because He knows best. Unfortunately, the gates of hell are being opened, and demons are coming into our world more frequently. The sad thing is some people are attacked innocently and some of those people are children or our elders. On the other hand, there are some people opening these doors intentionally to harm others or to gain power or favors from Satan.

I prayed for strength and guidance to follow this path I was being led down. I understand some people would say not to mess with things like this, but this was what I felt the Lord had brought my way. I believe He knew I would be strong and use logic to follow this spiritual warfare path. Just like in my mother's bathroom, I was not afraid. There was no reason for fear. However, I know many people that would have handled that situation differently. Demons gain power and feed on people's fear. I am not one to scare easily, especially knowing I have God guiding me. However, I am not stupid, which is where logic comes in. Abiding by the rules and laws in the paranormal field and the Bible were critical for the safety of myself, my family and all involved.

A Catholic priest and deacon were involved with another paranormal team and were not comfortable with the group. They were seeking a professionally run paranormal team to help Jesus through spiritual warfare. As an acquaintance they knew me well enough to know I was a leader, organized, had a professional demeanor to manage a team, and more importantly, they knew how much I love the Lord. They asked if I would head up and manage a spiritual warfare team. They said they would train me and anyone else involved with the team. I was honored to be asked, and headed up the team. I felt this was what the Lord had been leading me/us to do to help protect His children from the evil one.

The four co-founders were, me, a Catholic Vatican-sanctioned exorcist priest with more than 30 years' experience specializing in exorcisms, a deacon and demonologist whom the priest had trained for years, as well as a Catholic lady who also felt led to this team by God. The entire group eventually grew to 15 members, with each trained person having an important role in this spiritual warfare battle through the grace of our Heavenly Father.

Together the four of us built a wonderful, God-loving team. The group worked well together, and I strongly believe we were all chosen by God's hands to help individuals in dark situations. As well as innocent people grieving the loss of their loved ones who required spiritual guidance through their difficult times.

In the 11 years of our spiritual warfare service through God, all m maintained a professional demeanor and shared strong religious values, even though we were from multiple denominations. Some of our more serious cases involved: voodoo, black magic, curses, and other Occult practices.

Everyone was aware of the dangers of what we did and do in this nonpaying field. We never charged for helping others regardless of their financial status. We never asked for donations, but if someone wished to give us a donation, we would accept it, because all our equipment, frankincense, myrrh, and other incenses needed, plus many, many batteries, computers, tv monitors, and gas, among other things came directly from our own pockets. None of us were rich by any means. Donations helped supplement expenses. Could we have helped people in these dark situations? Absolutely not. If it weren't for our Lord guiding these people to us, if it weren't for His guidance and giving us the strength, and the right team members, we wouldn't have been as successful in resolution. Our reputation became recognized, and we were labeled the resolution team throughout the east coast. None of us took pride in the outcome of each case, it was clearly through the grace of God's hands. We prayed for protection before each investigation and thanked the Lord for allowing us to be an instrument for His glory.

Prior to any investigation we'd conduct a lengthy detailed intake background report of each person in the home or business. This document also included any mental or physical disabilities, among other pertinent questions. We'd also research the history of a property, and prior owners before conducting any physical investigation. Sometimes we would reach out to other nearby neighbors for additional background history.

In some cases, families needed to be educated about what they did to welcome in an entity. We've given lectures at public events and universities to educate people about the dangers of communicating with the dead. Nobody should be involved with the paranormal just to get a thrill or to experience something! Nobody should investigate their own home, especially alone. Teams need to educate themselves first and learn the paranormal laws and weapons used to help others in threatening situations. And how to protect themselves, their loved ones and those they are helping.

Our team's mission was to help people the Lord sent our way. In many cases after resolving our client's paranormal predicament, they would reconnect with their churches and in some cases, it brought some people to the Lord who didn't know Him.

CASE EXAMPLES OF GOD'S PATH

Case 1 - Sandy and Barry's Private Residence

Through our research we discovered something interesting from a local elderly neighbor. He said, *"Many years ago when I was a child, there were traveling gypsies living on the property. They were loud, disrespectful, and unruly. The people living in the area wanted them out. The property wasn't their land, and they had no respect for the people on the street nor did they take care of the land. Authorities came out and forced them off the property."* This critical information was key to solving this mystery. Not in most cases, but in some when gypsies were forced off a property, they would become quite angry and curse the property before leaving.

This was very important information none of the other teams obtained. We also learned there used to be a large home at the back of their wooded property. Tragically, the home burned down many years ago, and all family members perished inside. This occurred after the gypsies left the property.

With all the information gathered, we had a great suspicion that a demonic entity was summoned to the property, then trapped the souls of these spirits when they perished in the fire. These spirits were trying their best to communicate with the living to make themselves known to get the help they needed.

When we arrived at their home, we shared our interesting findings of the property's past, then explained our plan of action. We conducted a paranormal investigation and had incredible evidence through photos and audio of who and what was haunting their home. After the reveal, our entire team gathered around their dining room table with my mother and Barry. We never do seances, use Ouija boards, nor do I ever allow spirits to use my body to communicate. Our priest walked around their rectangular shaped dining room table multiple times reading a very powerful exorcism prayer.

During these times, the priest asks archangels, angels, and saints to intercede in helping cast out demons. At the peak of this powerful prayer, a bone-chilling, deafening thunder rumbled directly above their home. This demonic entity was very powerful, but no match for the Lord. On that night there were no storms, clouds or any type of predictions that could have otherwise been involved in what we heard. This was without a doubt a battle between Heaven and Hell, and all present could hear it as it occurred. Everyone was in shock, and all of us looked at each other silently with eyes wide open. Each case is different, but this one was unique because we were hearing the battle above us. Our priest never missed a beat as he continued with a stern voice delivering this exorcism prayer. It was an experience all of us will never forget. The curse was finally broken, and the spirits were no longer held captive by the entity. I'm sure the angels and saints helped guide them home to finally be with our Lord and their loved ones..

My mother and Barry still live in their home. They have never had another incident since that extraordinary night. Praise Jesus for answered prayers to protect my mom and Barry. We were also thankful for the archangels, angels, and saints interceding to remove the curse and cast out that powerful demonic entity.

Case 2 – Victims of a Past Owner

Much like the other case, four paranormal teams had investigated the home prior to our involvement. The second team suggested the family move. When we arrived, a for sale sign was on the property, which was sad to see, because we knew it was not necessary. The last team was a Christian group who reached out to a local exorcist priest who exorcised the home. The Christian team then reached out for our team's help because their attempt to have the house exorcised was unsuccessful. They were at a loss for bringing peace to this distraught young family's home. The family not only was being emotionally troubled, but also physically harmed, including the children.

Our priest contacted the previous exorcist priest. They knew each other, which was good. The priest shared the level of exorcism he used, which evidently wasn't high enough for the entity in this home. *(Yes, there are different exorcism levels for different demons. The more deeds they succeed in, the higher they climb in hell as they receive their reward of becoming more powerful.)*

The innocent young family had three boys: ages, 18 mos., a three-year-old, and a five-year-old. They were a very devout Catholic family who attended church regularly. Shortly after purchasing the home, they started experiencing paranormal activity. The children were being targeted to irritate the parents. After one of their boys was scratched, the mother yelled out, *"Leave my children alone!"* Immediately after speaking these words, she was scratched on her neck. Once the attacks became physical, they reached out for paranormal help.

> ***Just to let you know, there is a happy ending to this case. And please take note, physical attacks on people are very uncommon. Provoking could definitely bring on physical attacks, therefore we do not advise anybody or paranormal teams to provoke a demonic entity in order to get a reaction. Our team did take on some of the worst cases where other teams were not comfortable or educated to accept.***

We were convinced there was something sinister happening in this home. Before arriving we made sure we did our homework. After researching previous owners and the home's history, we discovered the previous owner was forced out of the home by his own children, who put him in a nursing home. We're not sure why they did it, however it's *possible* it was for their own financial gain. The home sold quickly at a reasonable price.

The angry previous owner was from a culture that sometimes puts a curse on people when they feel they've been wronged for one reason or another. So, we suspected there was a good possibility he put a curse on whoever bought his house. He probably didn't want someone else enjoying his home he so loved.

This case was a few hours away from our home base, and it wasn't too uncommon for us to travel a great distance to help a family, especially when children or the elderly were involved. Whenever we did an investigation, or exorcism of a home where children were involved, we'd ask the parents to have their children present when we arrived so Father could give them a blessing, then have someone take them during the investigation, like a friend or relatives' home to protect them during the spiritual warfare battle.

The previous Christian group asked if they could assist and observe our team to educate their team. They were a good team, and we knew we could always use the extra prayers. We allowed them to assist and observe our team. They were very respectful. Plus, we knew God led them to us and we had this opportunity to educate their team for future spiritual warfare battles.

In the end, our priest delivered an ancient exorcism prayer he felt compelled to use. The exorcism to banish this powerful demonic entity lasted over two hours. When we do an exorcism, we make sure we bless every nook and cranny, i.e., all rooms, porches, closets, attics, basements, fireplaces, and any other possible entries into the home or hiding spots. After this exorcism, all present could feel that the heaviness present in the home when we arrived had been lifted. The home felt peaceful and full of good energy. We knew the curse had been broken. It's interesting how a dark entity can bring on such negative heavy energy that can literally be felt by humans.

In this case, had the people moved, the entity most likely would have followed them. Why? The curse was directly on whomever bought the house. The ancient exorcist prayer father used was to remove the demonic entity summoned to the individuals who purchasing the home. Demons like to hide so we weren't taking any chances it was going to hid from the incense, and powerful biblical words, especially hearing Jesus Christs' name mentioned.

TESTIMONY TO THE BROKEN CURSE

When we arrived at this home, we could see the three-year-old and five-year-old boys were visibly scared. This demonic entity was torturing the children by showing them a hung man in a corner of their bedroom, and other horrific things no child should see. Before they left with a family member after Father blessed them, we gave them some holy water to spray the front door window and gave them some paper towels to clean the window. We told them they were cleaning the window so the angels could come in. They were not ornery, angry, or stubborn little boys. They were very young and innocent well behaved boys. So, when the mother emailed me a wonderful message, I believed her message to be a true statement. She said her five-year-old son told her, **"Last night Jesus and two angels were there and said we are going to be fine."** We appreciated this feedback because this witness was an innocent child. Two days later she emailed me again to say her son just told her the two angels were still there. We were thankful for the Lord and His two angel's miraculous approach to ease this child's nightmares.

Our team has observed many wonderful blessings, which has made all of our team members stronger in their faith.

Case 3 – An Innocent Family Plays the "Ouija Board Game"

We received a desperate call from a mother of five children who stated the children were petrified to go to sleep and some were reportedly being physically attacked. After speaking with the mother, I set up an appointment to visit the home to gain more information about their situation.

After interviewing the family, we discovered the point of the first activity. The family played with a Ouija board. The parents explained it was near Halloween, and they took the kids over to Delaware's *"Crybaby Bridge"* for the excitement of the upcoming holiday. *(Some states have their own Crybaby Bridge urban legend versions of the story.)* Here's their state's urban story; ***DE: The legend of the Crybaby Bridge"*** *https://donttalkjusttravel.com*

When they came home, they played the old-time family Ouija board game the father grew up with many years prior. They said they owned two old Ouija boards. They thought it was just done as an innocent fun game to play. The father said he never experienced any problems in the past, that's why he didn't question playing it with his kids. They alleged they thought the Ouija board was just a game and not dangerous.

The oldest boy of the five children was 16 at the time when he reportedly was attacked while doing homework on his computer; he had three scratch marks on his left arm. Some nights, their 11-year-old-daughter claimed to have been visited by a tall, dark, shadowy man leaning over her bed next to her as he/it watched her. She was so terrified she was unable to move when it was present. She'd cover her head with her blankets until it went away. This dark shadowy figure was seen by most of the family members at different locations inside the home. They all said they felt like they were always being watched, as did other family members and friends who visited them. Some people who saw the dark figure in the home refused to visit again.

Once, their 11-year-old daughter was caught in a room playing the Ouija board during the wee hours of the morning. When the mother found her daughter alone playing the game, she was shocked. She approached her daughter, and the child appeared dazed and claimed to have no idea how she got into the room and seemed dumbfounded that she was even playing the game. The mother said she fully believed the daughter didn't intentionally do this, and thought something evil was controlling her daughter. The mother added that she believed her daughter would have been too scared to be by herself, especially after suffering in fear of this shadowy figure huddling over her bed.

We treated this as an emergency case, since the dark threats towards this family were escalating, and more importantly, to protect the 11-year-old child, who seemed to be of great interest to this entity. We knew God led this family to us to help assist in protecting their daughter and everyone else in the home. Someone they spoke to about their dangerous situation heard about our spiritual warfare team and gave the father our contact information. They needed help. We spent time educating them about the dangers of the Ouija Board, and we left them protection prayers. We wanted them to feel safe in their own beds once again.

When Father blessed and exorcised the home, it took a little over an hour. Then we requested to meet with the whole family, including all five children to be present. We wanted to counsel and educate them about their experiences, as well as the dangers of playing with a Ouija board. We also gave them a chance to ask any questions or express concerns they had. We warned the children and parents, *"If you use the Ouija board again, or are anywhere near someone using the Ouija board, this entity will come back and things in their lives would be worse."* Everyone said they understood and agreed. The father allowed us to take his two family Ouija boards so they could be properly destroyed. Everyone vowed never to use one again.

About a year later, the father of this family called us again and wanted to know if we could come immediately. When we arrived, the parents were apologizing for troubling us a second time. We explained this was not a problem and asked how we could help. We could hear the desperation in their voices when they spoke.

They started the conversation with… *"You were absolutely right about how things get worse if anybody plays or is around someone playing the Ouija board."* Then they told us why they needed us so urgently.

DARLENE M. LINK

The mother started first. We could hear the fear in her voice as she trembled while speaking. She stated she was scratched on her thigh while taking a shower, and said objects from the kitchen counter were being thrown across the room by an unseen force, among other things. All the children in the home were genuinely scared, and the parents also admitted they have never been more scared for their children, especially their now 12-year-old daughter. The most concerning details of their story were when their daughter went into their basement and was in a position to hang herself. They heard something in the basement and went downstairs to investigate the sound. That's when they discovered her. They explained it was as if their daughter wasn't in control of what she was about to do. The parents reached her in time, thank God, and started rushing her to a children's hospital to be psychologically evaluated. The girl was unaware of what she was doing until her parents frantically spoke to her, which broke the control by the entity. Their daughter began crying profusely on the way to the hospital and admitted to her parents why things were happening again in the home. She explained, *"When I went to (friend's name) house for a sleepover, the girls wanted to play the Ouija board."* She said, *"I told them I didn't want to play it, and I didn't. But the other girls still played it."* She also told her parents she tried staying as far away from the girls when they were playing it. So, when things started happening to her family, she said she was afraid to tell them, because she knew it was all her fault.

Now we understood the problem we were facing. Again, once a demon has been sent back to hell, then the game is played by the people or being played in the presence of their target, the entity is being welcomed back. So, each time the same demon comes back, it comes back stronger, more powerful, and aggressive. God wasn't having it. He led the parents to the basement and stopped her before this demon succeeded in his deed.

We knew we had our work cut out for us this second time around. After saying our protection prayers, *(as we did in all cases)*, our priest gave each one of us a blessing, including the clients. It was time to get started and we were prepared for battle.

I GIVE THIS TO YOU LORD

Our priest and deacon performed a higher-level exorcism on the home. The team and parents followed along as we all prayed together. Afterwards, everyone was exhausted, but the entity was gone. Every minute of this lengthy dangerous exorcism was worth the efforts we put forth to help this family.

After the home was cleansed a second time, the parents said they didn't think their children would ever play the Ouija board again or be around one. They also shared that they grounded their daughter for a long time. Education was important for all involved, especially the children that witnessed the destruction a demonic entity could do to them and the people they held closest to their hearts.

When we arrived, we had printed copies of each of these three powerful prayers to keep demons at bay: The Lord's Prayer; the Prayer for St. Michael the Archangel's intersession, and Psalm 91. The last we heard; the family was doing well. It's always important for us to leave these three prayers after ever case, as well as answer all questions they may have and educate where needed in each case situation.

I decided to include this story for people who are unaware of the potential dangers and evil associated with the Ouija Board.

THE OUIJA BOARDS IS NOT JUST A GAME

Using the Ouija board may seem innocent to some people or fun for college students, but this board is far from a game and it's especially dangerous when the users are under the influence of alcohol or drugs, depressed or mourning the loss of a loved one.

It truly is a portal to Heaven and Hell. There is a certain demonic entity connected to the Ouija board that can cause great destruction in people's lives, destruction beyond their wildest imagination. There are many other entities/demons that can enter this portal as well. Sure, some people could use the Ouija board for years and never have a problem, but then again, it only takes one time for a demonic entity to come through the board and cause havoc in someone's life. Just like in Case 3. That situation could have ended far worse had the parents not been available to save their daughter from hanging herself. We strongly advise people not to use the Ouija board.

Unfortunately, the Ouija board "games" are sold in the game section of most stores targeting our children. They even make them appealing for very young children and teens, such as, brightly colored pink with kittens, (still a Ouija board), multicolored geode dream catcher boards, Halloween Ouija boards, Goddess spirit Ouija boards, blue boards for boys, glow-in-the-dark boards with a pentacle star in the center and a warning that reads, **"Use with caution, portal to supernatural realm."** *There are also boards, designed specifically from some of the most popular TV series for kids. All of these designs are a ploy to pull children in, as if they were just an innocent game for the general child/family to play. This makes spiritual warfare teams sickened, because we know the dangers and have to go into these homes to fix the problems associated with these so-called, "games".*

The board does have rules, and if someone were to use the board, we deeply advise them to abide by the rules. **Definitely say "goodbye" every single time the board is used, before leaving it, and place the planchet in a separate location from the board, even in another room.**

Our blessed team has always worked well together and are close, like a family. Unfortunately, our priest had bad lungs and passed away from pneumonia-related complications. We miss him greatly. As a team, through our 11 years we've learned lifelong spiritual warfare lessons from him and our deacon. The team is currently inactive. We still have people calling for paranormal guidance, as well as spiritual guidance about the Lord.

ANOTHER USEFUL PROTECTION

My advice for yourself and your child(ren) is this: Through our research, we have logged each case involving individuals who were baptized versus those who were not baptized, and our findings revealed in nearly every case, those not baptized were the victims of demonic attacks. Not just children, but everyone of all ages. Don't just get baptized because you fear being attacked. Please get baptized when you are ready to profess your faith in Jesus Christ for salvation, when you are ready to obey and commit to Jesus' 10 commandments. He is all loving and He wants to save everyone from the dark forces.

Jesus spoke of baptism as a second birth (regeneration), saying,

> **John 3:5** *"Truly, truly, I say to you, unless one is born of water and the Spirit, he cannot enter the kingdom of God".*
>
> **(Titus 3:5) St. Paul tells us that this new birth through baptism is salvific, stating that God** *"saved us, not because of deeds done by us in righteousness, but in virtue of his own mercy, by the washing of regeneration and renewal in the Holy Spirit"*
>
> **1 Peter 3:21** *"Baptism . . . now saves you, not as a removal of dirt from the body but as an appeal to God for a clear conscience, through the resurrection of Jesus Christ."*
> *https://www.catholic.com/qa/how-baptism-saves-u*

This chapter can't end without expressing our love for the Lord through our work in the Spiritual Warfare field. We give all Glory to God for leading us, protecting us and our families, and for protecting our clients and their families. As well as opening the hearts of the individuals who came back to Him and their churches after resolution of their desperate situations.

CHAPTER 14

SURVIVING THE OHOOPEE RIVER

On a completely different topic from the plan the Lord revealed to me is an exciting experience I had with my daughter. This chapter is very important for me to share because it was my first adventure after my miraculous healing. I had been away from enjoying life for several years, and now I was ready to break lose and enjoy all the senses nature offers once again.

It was my first trip since my healing to a small quaint city in Georgia where our daughter Stephanie and her friend Jason lived at the time. I only visited them one time prior. I realized the 12-hour trip from Delaware was too much for me to handle while I was ill.

During my previous visit, I knew Stephanie and Jason saw the pain I was experiencing and how difficult it was for me to participate in any activities with them. I'd have to take naps because I couldn't stay awake. Stephanie would say, *"It's ok, Mom, you just get some sleep, and we'll talk later."* I always felt bad sleeping when I had limited time to share with them. This time, I was anxious to show them the new healed me! It's different just hearing the words, *"I've been healed by the Lord and I'm feeling great!"* than to visibly witness the power of this majestic healing. I wanted them to see it first-hand, so they didn't have to worry about me anymore. This adventurous trip was going to be much different from my last trip. Stephanie and I had been counting down the days with great anticipation prior to my arrival. With Stephanie being the master of plans, I permitted her full responsibility to select the itinerary.

While traveling alone by plane, I was excited to be pain free, stress free, anxiety and depression free. I was thoroughly enjoying my window seat view that John insisted I have for my trip. As I gazed out the window, I could see the luminous sun rays shining through the majestic clouds. To me, everything was so magnificently beautiful since my healing! Thank you, Jesus for opening my eyes, ears, and heart.

When the plane landed, I was thrilled to be pain free to enjoy grabbing hold of Stephanie tightly with a big warm hug. This is one of the things I missed most, giving big hugs to my husband, and to all our children without pain.

After putting my luggage in her car, Stephanie immediately told me some of the plans for that day. It was going to be a pleasant sunny day, perfect for touring Savannah.

Much like Stephanie, I looked forward to punching through the itinerary Stephanie methodically planned for us during my stay. Some of the plans included outdoor activities, which I was looking forward to since I had spent so much time indoors when I wasn't well. I was looking forward to participating in something wild and crazy now that I felt alive again!

There was so much to do in just a little over a week, but we managed to do it all. Jason unfortunately had to work during the days, so when day two offered a beautiful sunny day, Stephanie and I decided to venture on a kayaking trip through the natural surroundings of the Ohoopee River. What we hadn't realized at this point was that we had forgotten to pack our life jackets on what would be one of the most dangerous, adventurous days of our lives.

When we approached the river, we couldn't believe our eyes. Stephanie said she had never seen the river's level so high. For several days prior to my arrival, the area had been hit pretty hard with heavy rain, so the water level was nearly halfway to the top of the trees that bordered the woods along the river in that area. Pondering *"should we, shouldn't we,"* we decided, *"We should."* There was a gently moving current that didn't appear to be threatening. So, we made a poor decision to venture out, especially when we realized at the last minute we didn't have our life jackets. Overly confident and excited about going on my first adventure since the healing, I realize how I *was not* being responsible, especially without the life jackets. We both thought it was something we could easily handle. Here we were, preparing for our launch into the river. We added all the necessities to each of our kayaks. Our cooler was on my kayak for a midway picnic, Stephanie had a beach towel for each of us, and Stephanie's properly protected cell phone was in her kayak. We gently pushed off and jumped into the kayaks without getting our feet wet. The sun's rays were bright and warm. Stephanie said it was the warmest day of the week. I still brought a sweatshirt in case the temperature changed before we got back.

Through our journey, Stephanie kept clueing me in about what the area's natural surroundings should look like, such as beach areas that were completely covered by water and the camping place where they and their friends would camp, as well as other familiar landmarks they and their friends would frequent, plus, some of their friends' homes along the river.

After paddling through the river for about an hour and a half, we decided it was time to find a stopping point to take a break and have lunch. When we went around a river bend, Stephanie recognized one of her friends' homes and said that it would be a great place to stop for a while. She knew these friends very well and knew they wouldn't mind us pulling alongside their property to have our lunch, even though they were working at the time of our visit. She said she'd let them know we stopped by later. We were sure they wouldn't mind, especially under these circumstances.

So, we paddled over to the few steps we could see out of about ten that normally would be visible. When we grabbed the railing of the steps, we had to put our feet into the water to pull our kayaks close enough to tie them up. We were only wearing flip-flops on this trip. The current was a little swifter, so we knew we had to do a great job of securing the kayaks. We didn't want to lose one.

The moment our feet touched the step, we both shrieked from the extremely cold water. We had no idea the water would be so briskly cold, and we even said the water felt like hypothermic temperatures. I've never felt water so cold, not even in the ocean.

Once the kayaks were secured, we unpacked our picnic food. Stephanie sure made some good turkey, tomato, lettuce, and cheese sandwiches. We each had peanut butter crackers, an apple, and water. It was peaceful and at that point all seemed to be going so smoothly. Stephanie decided this was a decent time to pull out her cell phone to let Jason know how things were going. Now let me share how secured this phone was: Stephanie wrapped the cell phone in many paper towels, then put it in a zip secured bag, then placed that in a leak-proof container intended for outdoor sports, with yet another large zip secured bag around the sealed container. She wasn't taking any risks of her phone getting wet—something for which we were very thankful later. As Stephanie was speaking with Jason, she explained to him how well things were going. He was genuinely happy for us and wished us a good time, but before saying good-bye, Jason warned us to be really careful with the water being so high.

After their conversation, Stephanie and I just sat, relaxed, soaked up the beautiful sunny day, and enjoyed each other's company with some small talk that was always important to us. Even though the sun was out, and we did have bathing suits on, we could feel the cool air coming in. I put my sweatshirt over my bathing suit just before we left the steps. Stephanie was still just in her bathing suit, but said she was comfortable. We cleaned up our picnic trash then put it in the little cooler on the back of my kayak. We climbed back into our kayaks and as we cruised past Stephanie's friends' house, the neighbor was barbequing and gave a nice hello and waved to us. His little excited dog was happy to see visitors and began barking a friendly bark. The gentleman shouted out to us, *"Be careful out there!"* We simultaneously replied, *"We will."*

A little while after leaving our beautiful picnic spot, we were heading for another bend in the river. As soon as we went around that bend, we feared the huge challenge before us. The current seemed to be moving

I GIVE THIS TO YOU LORD

swifter at that point as we headed straight for an uprooted tree that had fallen from the right side of the river. It was so enormous it nearly stretched across the entire width of the river. Because we were moving so quickly and it was in such close proximity to our kayaks, we really didn't have much time to think out our strategy to handle this situation. Nonetheless, we both used our paddles rowing as fast as we could to get away from the monstrous tree.

I immediately selected to go to the right because the water was pulling my kayak in that direction, which proved not to be the best direction to take. My kayak got hung up on a mound where a large branch from that tree protruded. Stephanie, being stronger to fight the river flow proceeded to the left side, then looked over at me to find I was stuck. Stephanie abruptly changed her direction with a quick maneuver to come to my aid. Unfortunately, it just wasn't quick enough for her to gain full control once her kayak began taking on water. The force of the water filled her kayak and Stephanie fell into the frigid water. She gasped trying to pull herself out of the icy water. I saw the large bag with the cell phone and yelled out to her, *"Grab the phone!"* She instantly grabbed the large bag and gracefully swung it overhand and onto the mound of debris of this massive tree branch I was stuck on.

Fear went through me when I looked at Stephanie trying to save the kayak and I saw her head barely above water. I could see the fear in her wide eyes and her whole head was nearly under the mound, which most likely had large branches that she could have easily got caught on. With great fear I knew she didn't want to lose her kayak, and I shouted loudly, *"Let go of the kayak!"* She said, *"I'll lose the kayak."* I continued shouting, *"It's ok, let it go, I don't want to lose you!"* Her head was just about to go under when she let go of the kayak. Deep down in the water it went, it took a while before it popped up on the other side of this tree. It kept going farther down the river until it was out of sight.

Knowing how cold the water was, the first immediate thing was to get her out of the water as quickly as I could. Everything happened so fast; it felt like an eternity to get her up and out of the freezing water. She was so cold her entire body was shivering out of control, and I could see goose bumps all over her arms and legs. I think for a couple minutes I was in shock because here was my daughter, cold as ice, and I'm wearing a sweatshirt over my bathing suit. She said calmly but shivering, *"Um, can I have your sweatshirt?"* I said, *"Oh my gosh, of course, I'm sorry, I should have thought of that right away."* I stripped it off as quickly as I could, then immediately she put it on. I still had the vision of nearly losing my daughter under the spider web roots of this massive tree.

Despite the situation, we still managed to laugh at ourselves; or maybe it was just laughter of hysteria. Stephanie was now sitting part way on the branch with her legs slightly dangling in the water because of the minuscule amount of space she had available. We both knew the kayak I was sitting on was a one person kayak and probably would tip over if she tried to get on it. And her body would be too heavy to sit on the blanket like mound of debris that surrounded the branch on which she was sitting. However, this was where she had carefully and successfully tossed her cell phone.

The mound moved like a wavy waterbed with any pressure on it. It was the formation of everything floating in the river, like loose pine needles, twigs, and all kinds of other natural particles passing by in the rapidly running water. The worst thing about this natural bed of debris was that it was infested with ants and spiders still trying to survive. Unfortunately, they were crawling all over us the entire time we were docked up against the distressed tree. These ants weren't friendly either; we were bitten several times while shoving them and the spiders off our bodies. This alone is a memory that will be embedded into our brains forever; it would be a nightmare to most people, even if they didn't have arachnophobia, *(fear of spiders)* or myrmecophobia, *(fear of ants)*. And with my past rheumatic fever hallucination experiences of spiders, I wasn't thrilled to be reunited with them once again.

Now that Stephanie had a sweatshirt on and was as steady as she could be on the branch, she reached down to get the bag with her well-packaged cell phone. She dialed Jason's phone and when he answered, she calmly and softly said, *"Hey, how are you? Are you having a good day?"* I wanted to burst out in laughter, because I thought she was going to be more hysterical. But she wasn't, she was so calm and tried not to shiver while she spoke. And I could hear his southern voice ask, *"So how y'all ladies doing?"* Stephanie, still using her calm voice, *"Well, not so good. I lost my kayak and my oar and I'm sitting on a branch freezing."* Then she illuminated all the details of what led to where we were. Without hesitation he said, *"Ok, I'll go by the house and get my kayak. Approximately where are you now?"* Stephanie told him, *"We are slightly down from the beach area where we camp with our friends."* Stephanie asked him if he thought we could travel with two people on the kayak I was using. He said, *"Absolutely not, it's made for one person; it would be too risky to have two people riding on it."* He asked, *"Is there any way you can swim to the side?"* Stephanie said, *"There is no way I can go back into the water, it is way too cold."* She also said, *"I'm freezing where I am now. I can't get my whole body out of the water and we're getting bitten by the ants and spiders on an infested mound around the branch I'm sitting on."* She let him know we were going to try two people on the one person kayak. He said, *"Ok, but be very careful and I'll be there as soon as possible."* They hung up after sending their love to one another. Jason had to leave his work to rescue us. Stephanie repackaged her phone, should we need it again.

Now, if you can, picture my long-legged, 5'7" slender daughter standing up on this sideways tree branch while we coached each other on how to get her secured on the kayak without tipping over in the rapidly flowing freezing water.

First, we decided she needed to be in the front to paddle the kayak. Stephanie had much more experience kayaking than I. Sounds simple, but it was not an easy task. For her to get in front of me, I had to gently slide forward for her to get a foot on the back of the kayak seat, then she took her other leg over my head, so I could begin to slowly slide back, but not too far because her other leg was still there. Once she planted her foot on the front of the kayak, she swung her other foot over my head. And then I could slide all the way back to the seat's back rest for Stephanie to sit down in front of me. We both have never moved so slowly and so gracefully before, but it worked. She was on and we were balanced.

Before taking off Stephanie asked, *"Can we say a prayer before we go?"* I said, *"Of course, we need to pray."* We bowed our heads, made the sign of the cross and I led this prayer, *"Lord God, we ask for the intercession of your angels today to help us get home safely, and to guide us during the rest of our journey. We also ask for Jason's safety as he travels in the water to rescue us. We ask all this in your name, Jesus Christ."* Then we made the sign of the cross again, and said, *"Amen."*

We very slowly and gently pushed off the branch and proceeded in the direction the kayak was facing. We had no choice but to go to the right of this massive tree. There was a large enough opening for us to get through, however, we had to bend our bodies slightly to get under the tree itself. I told Stephanie I was going to relax my body to go in the movement of the kayak so I wouldn't go against her body movement. I knew enough about physics to know if I went in the opposite direction of her body movement, we could easily tip over. The kayak was very sensitive to movement with the weight we had on it. Stephanie was doing a great job keeping control as she paddled, and I kept saying as I nearly sung these words very softly and slowly; *"I am... the kayak. I am... the kayak,"* while my body relaxed and swayed in whatever direction the kayak moved. After traveling around other tricky areas, we came across a long stretch of straight river with a bend up in the distance. Stephanie excitedly asked, *"Is that my kayak up there?"* I looked ahead and softly yet enthusiastically questioned, *"Whatever it is, it is yellow, so it could be!"* As we got closer, we could see it clearly was her kayak. We were ecstatic and hopeful that we may be able to get it back. But it was going to be tricky getting to it, since it appeared to be hung up in the thicket brush along the river's edge. We were in an area that had higher land for us to stop on the side of the river. It wasn't too far from her kayak, but not close enough to reach from the right side without difficulties.

Stephanie carefully drifted our kayak up to the right so we could get out. She got out at the edge first, then as soon as her feet hit the land, she let out a screeching sound, *"Ouch!"* She was stepping onto prickly holly leaves. Now, because Stephanie had lost her pair of flip-flops when her kayak tipped over, we had to share my pair of flip-flops. In addition to the prickly holly leaves, we had to deal with long wild rose vines with pointy thorns hanging down everywhere from the higher trees. Stephanie stayed right in her spot as I steadily got out of the kayak. We decided the best way to deal with the ground covered in holly leaves was to share the one pair of shoes we had available. We pulled the kayak up on the ground a little. Then with my flip-flops on, I pushed the holly pines out of the way so I could take off my flip-flops before stepping on the ground. I passed them off to Stephanie to put on so she could take a few steps ahead. Then she would toss them to me so I could catch up, then to her and to me, and so on, until we got to the edge where we would attempt to get her kayak.

  We looked at each other and couldn't help but burst out laughing about our crazy situation. As if our mistake wasn't bad enough, from falling into frigid water and losing a kayak, an oar, the two towels that were on her kayak, and a pair of flip flops, we also were dealing with the biting ants, creepy crawling spiders, and now the prickly holly leaves, and thorny wild rose vines with one pair of flip-flops. We couldn't believe it, but we kept our spirits up and kept laughing at ourselves and the situations we were in. We had a lot of material to make plenty of jokes. Yes, we got scratched up a little, but the journey was just getting so ridiculous it was comical.

  We were amazed at how we both worked so well together, not freaking out or getting upset. We had fun with each other and knew we would get through this despite all our challenges. We tried to figure out a way to get her kayak from the very thorny area. It seemed impossible to get to it. Stephanie grabbed hold of a small tree and took my hand while I stretched out as far as I could, but it just wasn't enough to reach it. Then before our eyes, the kayak started to wiggle from side to side and backing out on its own. Then, as if being guided to us by an unseen force, it started floating in our direction to the edge where we could reach it. We were both mesmerized watching its movement. We agreed without a doubt and spoke it allowed, *"That was a miracle of the angels helping us."* The way the kayak moved was as if there were people in the water literally working it out of the wild brush and towards us. Amazing! If we hadn't seen it with our own eyes, we wouldn't have believed it. I'm sure people think we are embellishing the truth here, but it is absolutely what happened. We thanked the angels for their intercession through our Lord. We thanked our Lord for hearing our prayer and sending them to our aid. And as crazy as all of this sounds, it is all 100% true without fabrication.

The kayak still had a good bit of water in it. We tilted the heavy yellow kayak on its side to empty out as much of the water as possible. Then we lifted it to allow the rest of the water to drain out of the back of the kayak spout. It was a struggle lifting it, but we were determined to get the heavy water out and we did.

Feeling much better now that we had two kayaks, with still one oar, we were ready to get out of the unfriendly area. Stephanie hooked the two kayaks together with the kayak strap so she could paddle both vessels down the river with the only oar available to us. We pushed off, and away from the river's edge we went. With the two kayaks connected, it was important she swung wider around obstacles and river bends to successfully get both kayaks safely around them, especially where branches were hanging down from other smaller fallen trees. While working our way around the protruding branches, we would warn one another to duck. We were a great team.

Stephanie paddled a lot, and I knew her poor arms were getting tired. But, determined Stephanie kept going. Alas, we could hear Jason's voice shouting, *"Marco!"* As soon as we heard him, we both immediately responded, *"Polo!"* After a few more Marcos and Polos we were able to see each other. Our hero Jason had arrived. I'm sure he was glad he found us, especially since he had to paddle up the river against the current. He told us his truck was parked down the river a bit.

First, we had to get to the side of the river again so we could hook my kayak up to Jason's kayak to take the pressure off of Stephanie. In doing so, I lost my balance, tipped myself off my kayak, and into the freezing water I went. The kayak was fine, but I was beyond cold. When I fell into the water, I went completely underwater and sprang up quickly trying to get my chest out of the water. The water was so cold it took my breath away. I latched myself onto Jason's kayak the rest of the way until we reached the edge. I wasn't in the water for very long, thank goodness.

Once we got to the edge, we realized how prepared Jason was for his rescue of us. He brought extra dry towels, a shirt for each of us and life jackets. Stephanie stayed in my warm sweatshirt, while I was glad to take one of Jasons heavy shirts. We were so thankful he came equipped to handle the situation.

Now that my kayak was hooked up to Jason's, Stephanie was able to get back in hers. It was time to head back to Jason's truck. We traveled another couple miles before reaching our destination. It was such a relief the adventure was over. We were laughing at ourselves throughout this whole crazy experience. Jason was laughing at us and said he had to take a picture of us after we loaded up the kayaks on his truck. It was a blessing Jason was reachable and available to rescue us. And once again, we were thankful for the angels' help, and for the Lord hearing and answering our prayer. It truly was an exciting adventure—one we will never forget.

We looked forward to telling family and friends about this foolish adventure. I'm not proud to say we did it, but I'm proud to say we worked well together in our predicament as we survived the *"Ohoopee River Adventure!"*

DARLENE M. LINK

**Stephanie and Me
Ohoopee River Adventure**

CHAPTER 15

UNDERSTANDING GOD AND HIS LAWS

There are many reasons why some people do not know God and His laws. Some parents elect to not teach or practice any religion in the home. Some parents expose their children to so many different religions to let them pick their own when they get older, but that only confuses them. Some parents teach New Age practices, and then there are some parents who practice dark religions. Some parents use religion as a punishment, and then the children hate God for what was improperly forced on them. Some parents weren't taught as a child, therefore can't teach their own children. And there are some parents who were raised with religion, but are too lazy to commit to taking their children to church to get to know the Lord, which hurts the children in the long run for when they have their own children.

Some people may say, *"Oh, I've heard about the 10 Commandments,"* or *"I know there are seven deadly sins,"* but does everyone understand what they mean?

LAWS SET BY OUR LORD

Why do we have the 10 Commandments? Because people kept losing their way in life and faith by falling back into their sinful ways and sometimes extremely evil ways. God created the 10 Commandments to help remind us not to be sinful, but to mirror His image in loving all.

I wish every family would print and frame the Ten Commandments, then hang it in their home in a convenient location for their children to see. It could help the parent in raising their children to learn good Christian values.

THE TEN COMMANDMENTS:

I.   I am the Lord your God: you shall not have strange Gods before me.
II. You shall not take the name of the Lord your God in vain.
III. Remember to keep Holy the Lord's day.
IV. Honor your father and your mother.
V.   You shall not kill.
VI. You shall not commit adultery.
VII. You shall not steal.
VIII. You shall not bear false witness against your neighbor.
IX. You shall not covet your neighbor's wife.
X.   You shall not covet your neighbor's goods.

Free Printable Ten Commandments:
https://i.pinimg.com/736x/1c/de/53/1cde5310102adbd70826dc49d602c395.jpg

LIVING FOR GOD

1 John 2:15-16 Do not love the world or the things in the world. If anyone loves the world, the love of the Father is not in him. For all that is in the world—the desires of the flesh and the desires of the eyes and pride of life—is not from the Father but is from the world. And the world is passing away along with its desires, but whoever does the will of God abides forever.

> **1 John 5:19** *We know that we are from God, and the whole world lies in the power of the evil one.*

> **Colossians 3:2** *Set your minds on things that are above, not on things that are on earth.*

There are many verses in the bible, see https://www.openbible.info/topics/dont_love_the-world

To me this means God has made an appealing, beautiful base for us to enjoy while in this temporary home, but we are not to obsess over things that are unimportant. It's ok to enjoy the beauty of the world, but it's not important for us to have all the luxuries of material things in this world, or to lust over anything, whether it is other humans, oneself, or objects. What is important is what we do to help and protect others in this world by feeding the poor and nurturing the underprivileged by offering them aid in whatever form we can. And, most notably, we dedicate our lives to the Lord and emulate the kind of person we should be to spend eternity with Our Lord and Savior. In the bible Jesus mentions the two greatest commandments in His laws.

> **Mark 12:28-34 28** *One of the teachers of the law came and heard them debating. Noticing that Jesus had given them a good answer, he asked him, "Of all the commandments, which is the most important?" 29 "The most important one," answered Jesus, "is this: 'Hear, O Israel: The Lord our God, the Lord is one. 30 Love the Lord your God with all your heart and with all your soul and with all your mind and with all your strength." 31 The second is this: "Love your neighbor as yourself.' There is no commandment greater than these." 32 "Well said, teacher," the man replied. "You are right in saying that God is one and there is no other but him. 33 To love him with all your heart, with all your understanding and with all your strength, and to love your neighbor as yourself is more important than all burnt offerings*

> *and sacrifices." 34 When Jesus saw that he had answered wisely, he said to him, "You are not far from the kingdom of God." And from then on no one dared ask him any more questions.*
>
> *https://www.biblegateway.com/passages/?search=Matthew%2022%3A36-40&version=NIV*

In other words, if you kill, steal, or disobey any of the other commandments, you certainly could not be abiding by the two most important laws as mentioned above. Keep the Lord in your heart, mind, and soul. Think good thoughts always because He knows your thoughts too. If you think bad thoughts about others or about yourself, even if you never speak of those thoughts, He knows. He deeply loves you. *Take a moment to close your eyes and try to quiet your mind and feel His love.* Pray for protection for yourself, and pray for others.

Some people think they are not worthy of being helped, therefore, they do not pray for themselves. I know people who felt this way and it's hard for them to open up because of how they were raised or how guilty they feel about the things they've done. If you pray for forgiveness, repent of the wrong you've done, and do your absolute best not to repeat the sin, the Lord will forgive you. He has proven that in the Bible on many accounts with sinners. He is a forgiving God, but remember, He will know if your heart is pure, if your mind is sorrowful, and your soul is remorseful. God wants us to be kind, compassionate, understanding, and loving to all. If we abide by these things, we will please the Lord and share eternity with Him, as He promises.

In doing God's work, it's important we are not proud and boastful when we help others. It is not important what comes from us, because if it weren't for Him to give us what we have, we would not be able to help others. Just thank God you have been so blessed to help those less fortunate. We are to give all the glory to God, as I give the glory of this book to God. If not for Him,

I wouldn't have written this book. If it weren't for the angel who told me to write the book through His message, I wouldn't have written it. If it weren't for Him, I wouldn't be able to help others. If it weren't for Him I'd still be ill and in agony with 24/7 pain. Praise Jesus for listening to my heart, just as He will listen to us and help us when we call on Him when we are weak and can bear no more. Pay attention to the signs He sends. He is always by our side; how blessed we are.

United States Conference of Catholic Bishops usccb.org
Awareness of the End of Time.

> **Romans 13:11-14,** *11 And do this because you know the time; it is the hour now for you to awake from sleep. For our salvation is nearer now than when we first believed; 12 the night is advanced; the day is at hand. Let us then throw off the works of darkness [and] put on the armor of light; 13 let us conduct ourselves properly as in the day,* not in orgies and drunkenness, not in promiscuity and licentiousness, not in rivalry and jealousy. 14 But put on the Lord Jesus Christ, and make no provision for the desires of the flesh.*

Other examples of Laws to abide in.

THE 7 DEADLY SINS:

LUST: Lusting our own bodies to make them perfect, lusting over other persons' bodies, lusting the flesh of bodies is a great sin. Constantly lusting over flesh is a sin.

> **We learn this in these bible verses:**
> **Timothy 2:22,** *"But flee thou youthful lust desires; and pursue justice, faith, charity, and peace with them that call on the Lord out of a pure heart.*

Job 31:1, *I have made a solemn promise never to look with lust at a woman.*

Matthew 5:28, *But I say to you, that whosoever shall look on a woman to lust after her, hath already committed adultery with her in his heart.*

Philippians 4:8, *In conclusion, my friends, fill your minds with those things that are good and that deserve praise; things that are true, noble, right, pure, lovely, and honorable.*

James 1:14-15, *14 but each person is tempted when he is lured and enticed by his own desire. 15 Then desire when it has conceived gives birth to sin, and sin when it is full-grown brings forth death.*

1 John 2:16, *Everything that belongs to the world-what the sinful self-desires, what people see and want, and everything in this world that people are so proud of-none of this comes from the Father, it all comes from the world.*

- ❖ Self-control to lustful desires and controlling passion for the good of helping others.

PRIDE: Having excessive pride viewing oneself to be greater without regards to others.

We learn this in these bible verses:

Jeremiah 9:23-24, *23 "…let not the mighty man boast of his might, 24 but let him who boasts boast of this, that he understands and knows Me…"*

Proverbs 8:13, *To honor the Lord is to hate evil; I hate pride and arrogance, evil ways, and false words.*

Proverbs 16:18, *Pride goeth before destruction: and the spirit is lifted up before a fall.*

Romans 12:16, *Have the same concern for everyone. Do not be proud but accept humble duties. Do not think of yourselves as wise.*

Corinthians 13:4, *Love is patient and kind; it is not jealous or conceited of pride.*

Galatians 6:3, *For if any man think himself to be something, whereas he is nothing, he deceiveth himself.*

James 4:6-7, *6 But he gives us more grace. That is why Scripture says: "God opposes the proud but, shows favor to the humble." 7 Submit yourselves, then, to God. Resist the devil, and he will flee from you.*

- ❖ To control prideful desires, humility is needed by not allowing ego and boastfulness to take over. Give the Glory to God; after all, He is the reason you have been able to do the things you take pride in.

GREED: Excessively pursuing material objects/things and money.

We learn this in these bible verses:

Hebrews 13:5, *"Let your conduct be without covetousness; be content with such things as you have. For He Himself has said, 'I will never leave you nor forsake you'"*

Exodus 20:17, *Do not desire another man's house; do not desire his wife, his slaves, his cattle, his donkeys, or anything else that he owns.*

Proverbs 11:24, *The soul that blessed, shall be made fat: and he that gets drunk, shall be drunk also himself. Proverbs 28:25, The greedy stir up conflict, but those who trust in the LORD will prosper.*

Ecclesiastes 5:10, *He who loves money will not be satisfied with money, nor he who loves abundance with its income. This too is vanity.*

- ❖ Charity work to help others is a great place to start working on the sin of greed. Remember; always give the Glory to God, because He has made it possible for you to have so much to provide for others in need.

ENVY: Having an unhealthy penetrating desire to obtain what someone else possesses.

We learn this in these bible verses:

Proverbs 14:30, *A sound heart is life to the body, but envy is rottenness to the bones.*

Job 5:2, *Surely inpatients kills the fool and anger slays the simple.*

Psalm 37:1-2, *1 Do not fret because of the wicked; do not be envious of wrongdoers, 2 for they will soon fade like the grass and wither like the green herb.*

Proverbs 24:19-20, *19 Do not be provoked at evildoers, do not envy the wicked; 20 for the evil have no future, the lamp of the wicked will be put out.*

Ecclesiastes 4:4, *Again, I was contemplating all the labors of men. And I took notice that their endeavors are open to the envy of their neighbor. And so, in this, too, there is emptiness and superfluous anxiety.*

Galatians 5:26, *Let us not become arrogant, competing against one another, envying one another.*

James 3:14-16, *14 But if you have bitter zeal, and there be contention in our hearts: glory not and be not liars against the truth. 15 For this is not wisdom, descending from above: but earthly, sensual, devilish. 16 For where envying and contention is: there is inconstancy and every evil work.*

❖ Showing kindness towards others in need, superseding your desires can help with this sin.

GLUTTONY: Is excessively eating of food or of drink.

We learn this in these bible verses:

1 Corinthians 10:31, *Therefore, whether you eat or drink, or whatever you do, do all to the glory of God.*

Psalm 78:17-19, *17 But they continued to sin against him, rebelling in the wilderness against the Most High. 18 They willfully put God to the test by demanding the food they craved. 19 They spoke against God; they said, "Can God really spread a table in the wilderness?"*

Philippians 3:19-20, *19 Their destiny is destruction, their god is their stomach, and their glory is in their shame. Their mind is set on earthly things. 20 But our citizenship is in heaven. And we eagerly await a Savior from there, the Lord Jesus Christ,*

Proverbs 23:1-3, *1 When you sit to dine with a ruler, note well what is before you, 2 and put a knife to your throat if you are given to gluttony. 3 Do not crave his delicacies, for that food is deceptive.*

Proverbs 23:19-20, *19 Listen, my son, and be wise, and set your heart on the right path: 20 Do not join those who drink too much wine or gorge themselves on meat,*

1 Corinthians 3:16-17, *16 Do you not know that you are God's temple and that God's Spirit dwells in you? 17 If anyone destroys God's temple, God will destroy him. For God's temple is holy, and that temple you are.*

❖ To make yourself healthy and fit is to be able to help others.

WRATH: Wrath is a very strong anger full of hate towards others.

We learn this in these bible verses:

Romans 12:29, *Beloved, never avenge yourselves, but leave it to the wrath of God, for it is written, 'Vengeance is mine, I will repay, says the Lord."*

Psalm 37:8, *Refrain from anger, and forsake wrath! Fret not yourself; it tends only to evil.*

Proverbs 14:29, *Whoever is slow to anger has great understanding, but one who has a hasty temper exalts foolishness.*

Proverbs 15:1, *A gentle answer quietens anger, but a harsh one stirs it up.*

Ephesians 4:26-27, *26 Be angry but do not sin; do not let the sun go down on your anger, 27 and give no opportunity to the devil.*

Colossians 3:8, *but now you also must give up all these things: human anger, hot temper, malice, abusive language, and dirty talk.*

James 1:19-20, *19 You must understand this, my beloved: let everyone be quick to listen, slow to speak, slow to anger; 20 for your anger does not produce God's righteousness.*

- ❖ Before acting out or speaking harsh angry words, work on patients, for that is the cure to understanding God's love and the love for others. Being angry as you judge others is sinful because there is only one judge, God, whom is the only judge of all of His children.

SLOTH: Excessive laziness is a brutal failure to understand and utilize your own talents.

We learn this in these bible verses:

Proverbs 6:6, *Go to the ant, you sluggard! Consider her ways and be wise.*

Proverbs 10:4, *Being lazy will make you poor, but hard work will make you rich.*

Proverbs 13:4, *The soul of the sluggard craves, and gets nothing, while the soul of the diligent is richly supplied.*

Proverbs 19:15, *The Slothfulness casteth into a deep sleep, and an idle soul shall suffer hunger.*

Proverbs 24:33-34, *33 A little sleep, a little slumber, a little folding of the hands to rest, 34 and poverty will come upon you like a robber and want like an armed man.*

Romans 12:11-13, *11 Never flag in zeal, be aglow with the Spirit, serve the Lord. 12 Rejoice in your hope, be patient in tribulation, be constant in prayer. 13 Contribute to the needs of the saints, practice hospitality.*

Colossians 3:23, *Whatever you do, do it from the heart, as for the Lord, and not for men.*

❖ Enthusiasm and interest in other things, be proactive to work for your needs and for humanity.

WHAT IS A MORTAL SIN?

There are 3 conditions necessary to commit a mortal sin...

1. **Grave Matter:** *They act out essentially an evil or immoral sin, such as murder, rape, incest, perjury, adultery, human sacrifice, torture and so on.*

2. **Full Knowledge:** *They are aware that what they are doing or plan on.*

    doing is an evil or an immoral act.

3. ***Deliberate Consent:*** *The person is using their own "free will" to commit the evil or immoral act.*

However, if a person is being forced to commit an evil or immoral act, that is not a mortal sin. Example: If a parent or other authority figure is forcing a child to do something immoral, they may not know better. They may feel it's not right, but are being forced against their will to do it, therefore, they are not responsible for the immoral act. They also may fear for their life from a parent or other person forcing them to do an immortal act if they don't comply to doing the immoral tasks.

THE MESSAGE

Life isn't hard if we follow the two main commandments, which would be abiding in all Ten Commandments to follow the two most important commandments, according to our Lord. And if we keep our Lord shining in our hearts, we will be glorifying our Lord. It's important to focus on what messages the Lord is giving us. There is a plan for each of us and it will be revealed to everyone if it hasn't already.

Satan's pests are scouting to seek the ruin of souls every minute of every day. Everyone left on this temporary home is at risk if they do not follow God's rules but live unholy lives. However, if we live a life that follows the laws of God, and we involve ourselves in deep prayer, we would be defending ourselves from demonic attacks. Take action for yourself in the battles that surround us in today's world. Stay strong against the evil from people seeking powerful titles to control us. Get baptized once accepting the Lord as your Savior. Keep praying daily and with every opportunity, be available to help others to follow the same path.

God has led me to write this book to share my testimony of His love and healing power. Without our pure faith in Him, He cannot heal us. It has to be absolute soulful faith to know He can heal us. *Do you trust Him? Can you release it to Him?*

I GIVE THIS TO YOU LORD

He also wants all of us to lean on Him through our faith, especially with all the changes we are witnessing in our world today. Surely, we can't go on with our simple lives knowing heinous things are being committed daily by evil people all around the world. Pray for the souls of our people to know Christ. He wants us to take time in our day to pray for others struggling to find the Lord. Without the Lord in our lives, there is nothing. We should call on Him daily to heal our world and to keep us and our families protected. Pray for the children, men and woman being trafficked daily into wicked places to experience unthinkable crimes on their bodies and even death. Pray for the weak and helpless to be strong and stand for their convictions to do what is right to help themselves and others. Pray for your enemies to find Christ. Pray for the things that have been reversed to return back to being good again, such as for evil to be called bad and good to be viewed as good again. We need to go back to our godly ways. Without God in our life, we have a corrupt world.

Everyone has time in their day to lift up a few words of prayer; whether it's in our cars traveling to work or school, working out at the gym, in the morning or evening, or as a family. I'm sure we can find a time that works best for our schedule. And of all things, it will be noted when we depart from this world that we sacrificed a few minutes a day to pray unselfishly to our Lord. There are people who may appear not to have our Lord in their souls, but if they only have a mustard seed of Christ left in their soul, there is hope for that person to turn their lives over to Jesus Christ to be saved. We should never give up hope or surrender our faith to anybody, nor for any reason.

Faith of a mustard seed; **http://bible.knowing-jesus.com/topics/ Mustard-Seed**

> **Matthew 17:20,** *And He said to them, "Because of the littleness of your faith; for truly I say to you, if you have faith the size of a mustard seed, you will say to this mountain, 'Move from here to there,' and it will move; and nothing will be impossible to you.*

FINAL WORDS OF ENCOURAGEMENT

Our family lives by…

Romans 8:28 *"And we know that for those who love God all things work together for good, for those who are called according to His purpose."*

Psalms 34:18, *"Those who seek the Lord shall not lack any good things!"*

I pray for blessings to come upon all who read this book. I pray hearts will be opened, with faith and trust to be stronger with every day in believing God wants to heal each one of His children. This knowledge is a message from the Lord for all to know. It's now in each person's hands and hearts to make their miracle a reality. Surrender your fears, and ego, and ask for forgiveness for any sins, then lift your petitions up to the Lord. Release all worries of carrying the burden by letting it go. Lift it up to the Lord, surrender it to Him! Tell Him, *"I give this to You, Lord!"* Let it go…*Hallelujah, Hallelujah!*

> *"Thank you, Jesus, for hearing our prayers and desires. Thank you, Jesus, for removing our illnesses, as well as our pain and suffering. We believe in Your promises, we believe You can heal us. Lord, we give this to You with our heart, mind, and soul, through faith and trust in Your miracles!*
> *Thank You, Jesus! Amen"*

May God Bless Each One of You Through Your Healing Journey ~

ABOUT KHARIS PUBLISHING

Kharis Publishing, an imprint of Kharis Media LLC, is a leading Christian and inspirational book publisher based in Aurora, Chicago metropolitan area, Illinois. Kharis' dual mission is to give voice to under-represented writers (including women and first-time authors) and equip orphans in developing countries with literacy tools. That is why, for each book sold, the publisher channels some of the proceeds into providing books and computers for orphanages in developing countries so that these kids may learn to read, dream, and grow. For a limited time, Kharis Publishing is accepting unsolicited queries for nonfiction (Christian, self-help, memoirs, business, health and wellness) from qualified leaders, professionals, pastors, and ministers. Learn more at: https://kharispublishing.com/